Elliott Wave
Simplified

Elliott Wave Simplified

**Making Stock Market Profits With
R.N. Elliott's Simple Theory**

By Clif Droke

Marketplace Books
Columbia, MD

ISBN 1-883272-48-3

Printed in the United States of America.

Contents

Introduction

Many books have been written on the Elliott Wave Theory in recent years. Most of them concern the rudiments of the theory and perhaps an exposition on how the theory may be applied to forecasting market trends. Almost without exception, however, all of them present the theory in a rigid, mechanical manner and lay down certain rules that are presumed to be inviolate. What most of these authors have done is to take R.N. Elliott's original working theory—much of it hypothesis—and attempt to make a veritable law of it. They merely regurgitate what Elliott himself wrote about his theory of technical analysis in the 1930s and 1940s with no attempt at refining or expounding on these basic principles whatsoever.

It is almost tragic the way this incredible theory of market analysis has been left in its primal state for over 60 years with only marginal improvements made along the way. Any other theory of technical analysis would have long since been refined and embellished to conform to the ever-changing standards of today's fast-moving markets. Not so the Elliott Wave Theory. Because it is so singularly remarkable and unique in its import and application, few have felt the need to add to its precepts.

In the years since its discovery, the Elliott Wave Theory has proven its reliability time after countless time. It is, however, not without defect. It is because of these defects that this book has been written. We do not attempt merely to explain the theory as most other books on the subject do. Nor do we claim to have made "new discoveries" about the theory. Our purpose is to allow the reader to apply the Elliott Wave Theory to trading markets in a practical, profitable manner without having to rely on the traditional flawed methodology inherent within the tenets of the original working theory. Nothing but careful study and real-time market experience can accomplish this. In short, we aim within these pages to help the trader avoid the pitfalls that so many practitioners of the Elliott Wave Theory encounter.

In the following chapters we will introduce trading methods combining the Elliott Wave Theory with other methods of technical analysis in a manner that produces optimal results—a combinatorial chemistry, if you will. It is this element of dynamic symmetry that has been sadly lacking in the development of the Elliott Wave Theory which, when properly applied, promises to advance the theory far beyond its present state and make it even more venerable than it already is.

More than anything else, this book aims at removing much of the needless "clutter" and cumbersome rules that restrict its usefulness and to reduce it to its most rudimentary components. In short, we aim at presenting a streamlined, simplified Elliott Wave Theory.

It is our hope that in the chapters that follow the reader will gain a fresh understanding and appreciation of this remarkable theory and learn to apply it to his or her investment strategy with profitable results.

Chapter 1

The Basics of the Elliott Wave Theory

What exactly is the Elliott Wave Theory? In essence, it is a theory of price movement which states that the price of any given stock or commodity (which we will refer to as "securities" in the remainder of this book for purposes of brevity) in a free market will travel in pre-determined wave-like advances and recessions, in a semi-cyclical fashion. Simply put, it holds that prices of actively traded securities move in wave-like motions in an alternating pattern that normally involves three steps forward for every two steps back.

The Elliott Wave Theory is more than just a theory of price movement, however. It is above all a philosophy of human emotion and crowd behavior—a psychological theory. Like its predecessor, the Dow Theory, its basis is in the behavior of humans in the aggregate. Robert Rhea, the great exponent of the Dow Theory, described this in his book, *The Dow Theory*, as follows:

...the pragmatic basis for the theory, a working hypothesis if nothing more, lies in human nature itself. Prosperity will drive men to excess, and repentance for the consequence of those excesses will produce a corresponding depression.

Following the dark hour of absolute panic, labor will be thankful for what it can get and will save slowly out of smaller wages, while capital will be content with small profits and quick returns.[1]

The same could easily be said of the underlying basis of the Elliott Wave Theory.

We have stated that the Wave Theory was a descendant of Dow Theory, the first comprehensive theory of stock market analysis in the Western world. Before one can fully comprehend the Elliott Wave Theory one must have a working knowledge of the basics of Dow Theory. While we do not wish to bore the reader with a prolix explanation and history of this theory, we do nonetheless feel it necessary to briefly touch on it before introducing more fully the Elliott Wave Theory.

The man for whom Dow Theory was named, Charles H. Dow, one of the owners of *The Wall Street Journal*, did not actually designate his theory of stock market price movement as the "Dow Theory." That was done by his friend S.T. Nelson, who wrote *The ABC of Stock Speculation* in 1902. It was he who first attempted to explain Dow's methods in a practical manner.[2]

William Peter Hamilton, who served under Dow, carried on the study and interpretation of the theory through occasional editorial forecasts.[3] It was Hamilton who first refined the theory and organized it into an efficient working system. His book, *The Stock Market Barometer*, published in 1922, explained the Dow Theory in detail.

"Interestingly," notes Steven Achelis in his book, *Technical Analysis From A to Z*, "the theory itself originally focused on using general stock market trends as a barometer for general business conditions. It was not originally intended to forecast stock prices. However, subsequent work has focused almost exclusively on this use of the theory."[4]

The Dow Theory comprises six assumptions:

The Averages Discount Everything.

"An individual stock's price reflects everything that is known about the security. As new information arrives, market participants quickly disseminate the information and the price adjusts accordingly," writes Achelis. "Likewise, the market averages discount and reflect everything known by all stock market participants."[5]

The Market is Comprised of Three Trends.

Achelis states:

At any given time in the stock market, three forces are in effect: the Primary trends, the Secondary trends, and Minor trends.

The Primary trends can either be a bullish (rising) market or a bearish (falling) market. The Primary trend usually lasts more than one year and may last for several years. If the market is making successive higher-highs and higher-lows the primary trend is up. If the market is making successive lower highs and lower lows, the primary trend is down.

Secondary trends are intermediate, corrective reactions to the Primary trend. These reactions typically last from one to three months and retrace from one-third to two-thirds of the previous secondary trend. The following chart shows a Primary trend (Line A) and two Secondary trends (B and C).

Primary Trend A

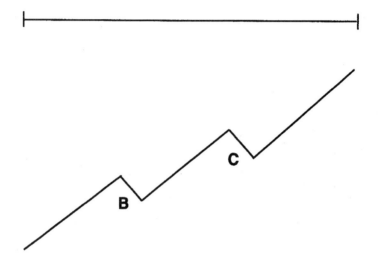

Minor trends are short-term movements lasting from one day to three weeks. Secondary trends are typically comprised of a number of Minor trends. The Dow Theory holds that stock prices over the short term are subject to some degree of manipulation (Primary and Secondary trends are not). Minor trends are unimportant and can be misleading.[6]

Primary Trends Have Three Phases

Robert Rhea summarizes for us:

There are three movements of the averages, all of which may be in progress at one and the same time. The first, and most important, is the primary trend: the broad upward or downward movements known as bull or bear markets, which may be of several year's duration. The second, and most deceptive movement, is the secondary reaction: an important decline in a primary bull market or a rally in a primary bear market. Those reactions usually last from three weeks to as many months. The third, and usually unimportant, move-ment is the daily fluctuation.[7]

The Averages Must Confirm Each Other

Our fourth rule of the Dow Theory is perhaps the most important one. For without confirmation of the "averages," (meaning the Dow Jones Industrial index and the Dow Jones Transportation index), a market trend cannot be considered 100% valid.

Expounding on this point, Hamilton wrote:

Dow always ignored a movement of one average which was not confirmed by the other, and experience since his death has shown the wisdom of that method of checking the reading of the averages. His theory was that a downward movement of secondary, and perhaps ultimately primary importance was established when the new lows for both aver-ages were under the low points of the preceding reaction.[8]

In other words, both averages must be traveling approximately (though not necessarily exactly) in the same direction within close proximity of one another in order to provide a Dow Theory confirmation of the prevailing market trend, whether up or down.

Volume Confirms the Trend

Our fifth tenet is not to be over-looked in importance, as it all too frequently is by Dow Theory practitioners. Although Dow Theory is based primarily on price action, volume should be used to confirm the primary trend.

Martin Pring, in his book, *Technical Analysis Explained,* writes concerning this rule:

The normal relationship is for volume to expand on rallies and contract on declines. If volume becomes dull on a price advance and expands on a decline, a warning is given that the prevailing trend may soon be reversed. This principle should be used as background information only, since the conclusive evidence of trend reversals can be given only by the price of the respective averages.[9]

A Trend Remains Intact Until it Gives a Definite Reversal Signal

Writes Achelis:

An uptrend is defined by a series of higher highs and higher lows. In order for an uptrend to reverse, prices must have at least one lower high and one lower low (the reverse is true of a downtrend).

When a reversal signal in the primary trend is signaled by both the Industrials and Transports, the odds of the new trend continuing are at their greatest. However, the longer a trend continues, the odds of the trend remaining intact become progressively smaller.[10]

A.J. Frost and Robert Prechter, in their seminal work, *Elliott Wave Principle*, called Dow Theory "the grandfather of the Wave Principle."[11] Indeed, the Dow Theory laid the foundation for the Elliott Wave Theory and there are many similarities between the two theories. Concerning these similarities, Frost and Prechter wrote:

The Dow Theory is essentially a wave theory based on the concept of similarity of action between the movements of the sea and the trends of the market. As Charles Dow once observed, stakes can be driven into the sands of the seashore as the waters ebb and flow to mark the direction of the tide in much the same way as charts are used to show how prices are moving. Out of experience came the fundamental Dow Theory tenet that since both averages are part of the same ocean, the tidal action of one average must move in unison with the author to be authentic. Thus, a movement to a new extreme in an established trend by one average alone is a new high or new low which is said to lack "confirmation" by the other average.[12]

Dow Theory laid the foundation for the Elliott Wave Theory. Without a firm understanding of its tenets and implications a student will not fully be able to comprehend or appreciate the Elliott Wave Principle.

Notes:

[1] Rhea, Robert, *The Dow Theory*, Fraser Publishing Co.,
   Burlington, Vt., 1993, orig. 1932, pg. 8
[2] Ibid, pg. 1
[3] Ibid, pg. 2
[4] Achelis, Steven, Technical Analysis From A to Z, Irwin,
   New York, 1995, pg. 116
[5] Ibid, pg. 116
[6] Ibid, pg. 117
[7] Rhea, pg. 32
[8] Ibid, pg. 71

[9] Pring, Martin, *Technical Analysis Explained,* McGraw-Hill, 1991, pg. 36

[10] Achelis, pgs. 120-121

[11] Frost and Prechter, *Elliott Wave Principle*, New Classics Library, Gainesville, Ga., 1978, pg. 175

[12] Ibid, pg. 173

Chapter 2

What is the Elliott Wave Theory?

The term "Elliott Wave Theory" is being used more and more in the vocabulary of traders and investors around the world today. The theory itself has been around for many decades and was popularized in the 1970s by Robert Prechter and A.J. Frost, through their book, *Elliott Wave Principle*. It has been learned by countless thousands of traders over the years and is increasingly incorporated in computer trading programs.

Despite all of this, however, there seems to be a very low comprehension of its tenets among traders and almost no consensus among practitioners of Elliott Wave Theory as to how the theory should be applied in order to best maximize profits. The aim of this book is to instruct the reader in the proper use of the theory for maximum profitability in almost any market. We will show you how to avoid the most common pitfalls that Elliott adherents encounter and how you can avoid the mistakes that most of the leading exponents of the theory make.

Before we do, however, we must lay the foundation for understanding Elliott Wave. It is essential that the analyst have a firm grasp of the basics of the theory and its application to financial markets.

In attempting to formally define the Elliott Wave Theory, we quote from Frost & Prechter in their seminal work, *Elliott Wave Principle*:

> *The 'Elliott Wave Principle' is Ralph Nelson Elliott's discovery that social, or crowd, behavior trends and reverses in recognizable patterns. Using stock market data for the Dow Jones Industrial Average (DJIA) as his main research tool, Elliott discovered that the ever-changing path of stock market prices reveals a structural design that in turn reflects a basic harmony found in nature. From this discovery, he developed a rational system of market analysis. Elliott isolated thirteen patterns, or "waves," that recur in markets and are repetitive in form, but are not necessarily repetitive in time or amplitude. He named, defined and illustrated the patterns. He then described how these structures link together to form larger versions of the same patterns, how those in turn are the building blocks for patterns of the next larger size, and so on. His descriptions constitute a set of empirically derived rules and guidelines for interpreting market action. Elliott claimed predictive value for the Wave Principle, which now bears the name, "The Elliott Wave Principle."*[1]

Broadly speaking, the Elliott Wave Theory (which we will henceforth abbreviate with EWT) can be summarized in the following statement, also by Frost & Prechter:

> *In markets, progress ultimately takes the form of five waves of a specific structure. Three of these waves, which are labeled 1, 3 and 5, actually effect the directional movement. They are separated by two countertrend interruptions, which are labeled 2 and 4...*

> *R.N. Elliott did not specifically state that there is only one over-riding form, the "five wave" pattern, but that is undeniably the case. At any time, the market may be identified as being somewhere in the basic five wave pattern at the largest degree trend. Because the five wave pattern is the overriding form of market progress, all other patterns are subsumed by it.*[2]

Basic Elliott Wave Pattern

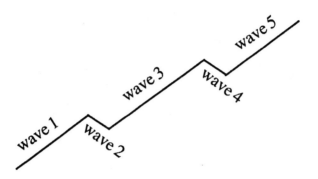

Before we can begin to discuss the nuances of the theory, it will be helpful to define a couple of terms that relate to EWT. There are two basic types of "waves" in any given market-impulsive and corrective. Impulsive waves are those price movements that are ascending in tandem with a rising trend or falling in a falling trend, while corrective waves are those waves that are falling counter to a rising trend, or rising in a falling trend. To provide for a better understanding of this, the following illustration should help:

Rising Trend and Falling Trend

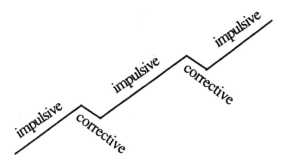

Falling Trend

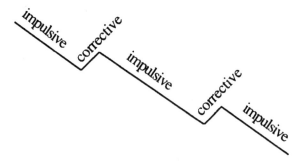

A completed Elliott Wave Cycle consists of five impulsive waves and three corrective waves:

Complete Elliott Wave Cycle

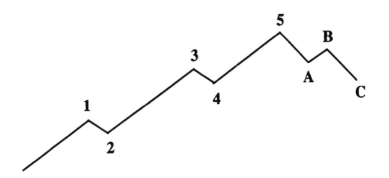

As you can see, the three wave "correction" is labeled "A-B-C," which is standard Elliott Wave taxonomy. So then, the primary assumption of the Elliott Wave Theory is that each movement, or wave, of a price trend consists of five components—waves one through five. These five waves are followed by three corrective waves.

The term "wave" itself has its origin from Dow Theory, as Charles Dow first made the analogy of stock market movements as compared to the waves of the ocean. In his book, *Elliott Wave Explained*, Robert Beckman observed that "the waves are subordinate to the tide, the ripples in the water subordinate to the waves, each rising and falling with rhythmic regularity, self-generated and forming cross currents, but the whole governed by seemingly moon-driven tidal forces."[3] Beckman further notes that this comparison illustrates the various trends of share price, "sometimes acting concurrently, sometimes running contradictorily, but always subject to an overriding force."[4]

Beckman summarizes the most important rules governing Elliott Wave Theory as follows:

1. For every action there is a reaction. Stock market movements in the direction of the main trend are impulsive moves. Stock market movements counter to the main trend are corrective moves. An impulse move is always followed by a corrective move.

2. Generally, all impulsive moves have subordinate waves while all corrective moves have three waves.

3. When the main trend is upward, waves 1, 3, and 5 are impulsive moves and waves 2 and 4 are corrective moves. When the main trend is downward, the first and third waves become impulsive moves, while the second wave becomes a corrective move.

4. The action of the main trend can be taking place over a time frame of anything from a few hours to many years.

When the main trend has completed a series of five waves, it reverses and a counter move of three waves is expected.

5. When completed, a move comprising five waves followed by a counter move consisting of three waves is the first cycle movement. This complete cycle movement will represent the first and second waves of a cycle in the time frame of the next higher degree.[5]

The Elliott Wave Theory is multifractal in nature, which is defined as a geometric shape that can be separated into parts, each of which is a reduced-scale version of the whole.[6] The multifractal nature of the Elliott Wave Principle is illustrated below:

Multifractal Elliott Wave Chart

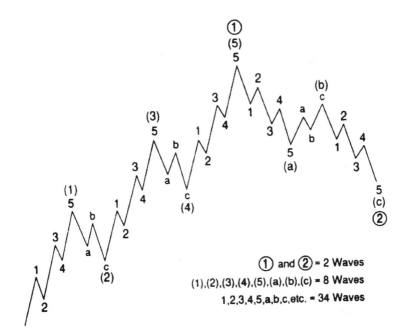

① and ② = 2 Waves
(1),(2),(3),(4),(5),(a),(b),(c) = 8 Waves
1,2,3,4,5,a,b,c,etc. = 34 Waves

In a nutshell, the Elliott Wave cycles can be numbered as 5-3-5-3-5-5-3-5. Elliott Wave Theory postulates that, regardless of size, a complete stock market cycle comprises eight movements.[7] Those eight movements comprise the first five impulsive waves and the first three corrective waves of a market cycle (see illustration).

Eight Movements of an Elliott Wave

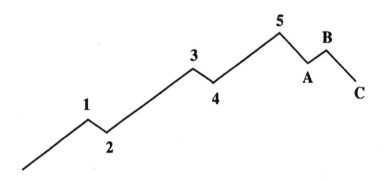

At this point, the theory gets a little more complex (and fascinating). Since Elliott Waves are multifractal, each individual wave subdivides into a further series of waves identical in form and number to the overall larger pattern of 5-3-5-3-5. For instance, wave 1 of a given impulsive Elliott Wave pattern subdivides into 5 additional waves. Of these five subdivided waves, a further subdivision is found which corresponds to the larger pattern in Pandora's Box fashion. Wave 2 subdivides into three "A-B-C" waves, and so on.

Break of Wave Patterns

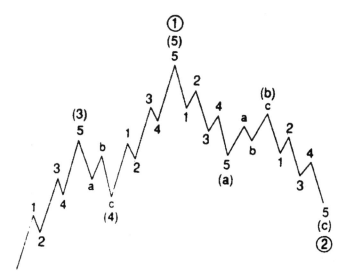

These subdivided waves are classified according to cycle degree. In formulating this theory, Elliott labeled each of these cycles, from the very smallest to the largest. The standard Elliott Wave classification—from greatest to least—is as follows:

Grand Supercycle

Supercycle

Cycle

Primary

Intermediate

Minor

Minute

Minuette

The largest of these wave cycles, Grand Supercycle, can typically be said to encompass 100 years or more. Each subsequent cycle classification encompasses a progressively smaller timetable up until the Minuette cycle, which can last from a few hours to a few days. Elliott even went one step further and christened a class of waves in the "subminuette" category, which typically last for only a few minutes or less. For all intents and purposes most traders may disregard this class of waves as it is normally too inconsequential to merit tracking.

In fact, as we will explain later in the book, traders will do well to ignore every wave cycle classification except for the minor, intermediate, and to a much more limited degree, the primary cycles.

A numerical system for labeling wave progress was created by Elliott and further refined and modified years later by Robert Prechter, editor and publisher of *The Elliott Wave Theorist*.[8] For academic purposes we include the wave labeling system here, but we will largely ignore it for the remainder of the book; thus, it is not necessary for the reader to memorize this system.

Wave Degree	5s With the Trend	3s Against the Trend
Supercycle	(I) (II) (III) (IV) (V)	(A) (B) (C)
Cycle	I II III IV V	A B C
Primary	(1) (2) (3) (4) (5)	(A) (B) (C)
Intermediate	(1) (2) (3) (4) (5)	(a) (b) (c)
Minor	1 2 3 4 5	A B C
Minute i ii iii iv v	a b c	
Minuette	1 2 3 4 5	a b c

Before closing this chapter it is necessary to delineate the basic rules of the overall Elliott Wave structure. They are as follows:

1. A cycle may not be said to be complete until a 5-3 pattern is traced out.

2. Waves are measured by distance covered on the chart (in terms of share price), not by time. (Time is relatively unimportant in our study of Elliott Wave Theory).

3. Concerning the requisites for wave lengths it is sufficient to note that wave 3 in an impulsive 5-wave move is usually the longest wave of the 5 waves, and *never* the shortest.

4. Of the three impulsive waves in a 5-wave sequence (the other two being corrective) two of the three waves tend toward equality, usually, but not always, waves one and five.

Equality of Waves 1 and 5

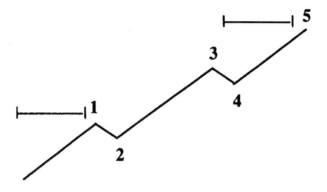

5. In like manner, waves two and four tend toward equality (in terms of distance covered).

6. In a clear rising or falling trend, the bottom of wave four must never penetrate the bottom of wave two; otherwise your wave count is incorrect.

Incorrect

Correct

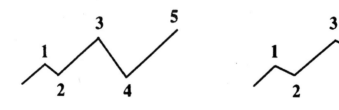

7. In many unfolding waves, the 4th wave reaction (also known as "corrective") is equal to the 1st wave impulse. Similarly, the 5th wave impulse is often equivalent to the 2nd wave reaction.[9]

8. In corrective moves, waves A and C of the A-B-C correction tend toward equality in most instances.

Equality of Waves A and C

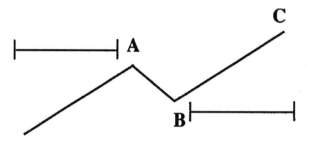

9. Wave B of the A-B-C correction must never penetrate below the bottom of wave A.

10. A-B-C corrections, regardless of where they occur in a wave sequence, typically retrace one-third of the previous 5-wave sequence. A-B-C corrections tend to stop at the *bottom* of wave 4 in upward trends and at the *top* of wave 4 in downward trends.

Nature of A-B-C Corrections

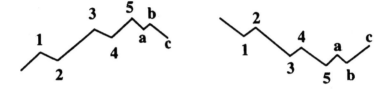

11. Fourth waves frequently take the form of a consolidation and often take the form of triangles or pennants on the chart.

Triangle Pattern in Fourth Wave

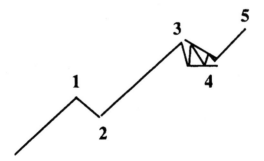

Triangle Pattern in Fourth Wave

While by no means providing a comprehensive explanation of all the nuances of EWT, this chapter lays out the basic tenets that will enable the beginning student to grasp the theory and apply it with at least some success. It will also help the intermediate-to-advanced Elliott students brush up on the basics and perhaps even gain new insight. In the chapters that follow we will delve into greater detail.

Notes:

[1] Frost and Prechter, *Elliott Wave Principle*, New Classics Library, Gainesville, Ga., 1978, pg. 19

[2] Ibid, pg. 21

[3] Beckman, Robert, *Elliott Wave Explained: A Real-World Guide to Predicting & Profiting from Market Turns,* Probus Publishing, London, 1995, pg. 24

[4] Ibid, pg. 24

[5] Ibid, pgs. 25-26

[6] Mandelbrot, Benoit B., "A Multifractal Walk Down Wall Street," *Scientific American*, February 1999, pg. 71

[7] Beckman, pgs. 6

[8] *The Elliott Wave Theorist*, P.O. Box 1618, Gainesville, GA 30503

[9] *Eric Hadik's INSIIDE Track*, January 1999, Vol. VII, No. 6, pg. 5, P.O. Box 2252, Naperville, IL 60567

Chapter 3

Corrections

Perhaps the single most difficult aspect of the Wave principle to learn is the identification of various corrective moves in markets. While the basic five-wave impulsive pattern character-istic of all impulsive moves is fairly simple to master, the label-ing of corrections is more difficult and requires greater study on the part of the student (otherwise known as an "Elliottician").

Unfortunately, this is also the most important aspect of the Wave Theory since the market (any market) generally spends from 60 percent to 75 percent of its time in some sort of cor-rective pattern. Thus, it is incumbent upon us to learn the nature of these corrections.

Zigzags

The first pattern we will take up is actually a variation of the basic three-wave A-B-C declining pattern, called a "zigzag" due to the appearance it takes on the chart. Zigzags can occur as many as three successive times on a chart but usually occur only once. The pattern is fairly easy to identify.

Zigzags

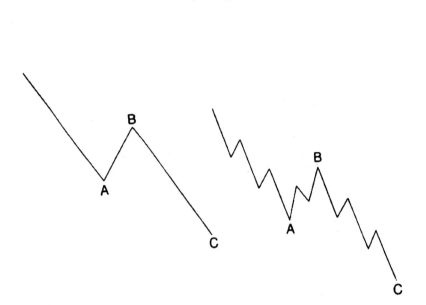

Flats

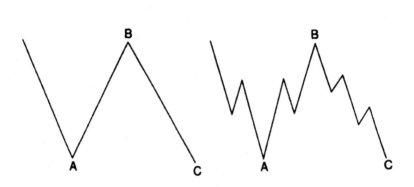

Another type of correction—a "flat" correction—as its name implies, takes on a flatter appearance than its "zigzag" counterpart and hence retraces less of the preceding impulse waves than do zigzags.[1] Flats cover much less distance than do zigzags and generally terminate just slightly beyond the end of wave A rather than significantly beyond as in zigzags.[2]

Triangles

Our final classification of corrective patterns are the triangles. Triangles represent the relative balance between buyers and sellers in a given market and can be identified on the chart by their triangular appearance (which almost always forms on diminishing volume). Rather than enter into a lengthy explanation of the characteristics of these patterns, we have printed the following chart,[3] which should aid the reader greatly in learning to recognize them.

Basic Corrective Patterns

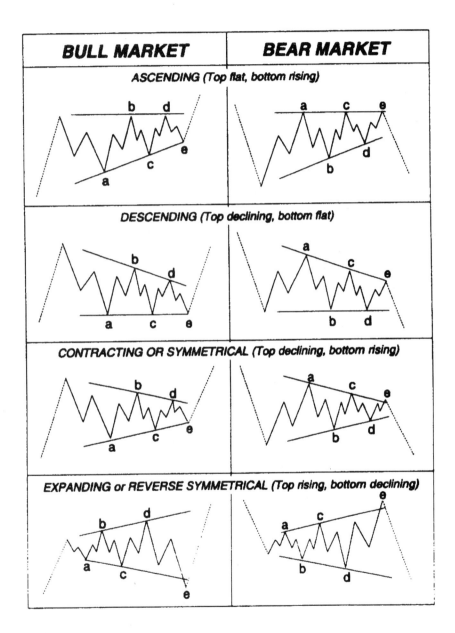

As you can tell, each triangle correction corresponds to the "Rule of Five" identified by technical analyst R.W. Schabacker, wherein prices are expected to alternately touch the upper and lower boundaries of a trading range a total of five times before breaking out from the triangle decisively. Furthermore, a measurement of how far prices will carry once they have broken out of the triangle is provided by measuring the widest ends of the triangle and adding the distance between them (in terms of price) onto the price level at the time of the breakout. It is also helpful to remember that prices generally carry onward in the direction they traveled prior to the triangle consolidation.

Classic Elliott Wave Theory has developed a far more sophisticated system for identifying the many types of corrections that we have covered here. We have omitted these additional techniques purposely, for we believe it is far too cumbersome and unnecessary to learn them. A simple overview of the basic corrective patterns such as we have provided here will suffice.

Triangles

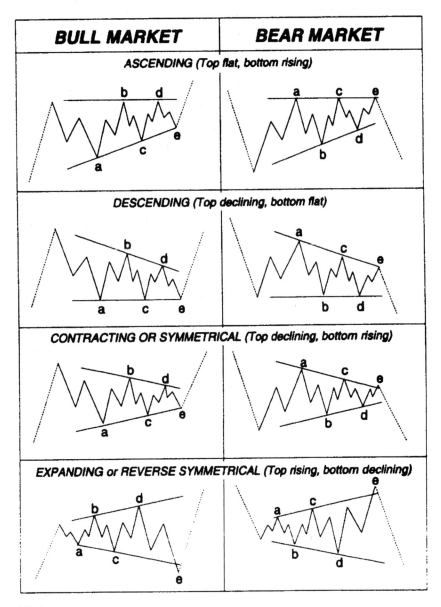

BULL MARKET	BEAR MARKET
ASCENDING (Top flat, bottom rising)	
DESCENDING (Top declining, bottom flat)	
CONTRACTING OR SYMMETRICAL (Top declining, bottom rising)	
EXPANDING or REVERSE SYMMETRICAL (Top rising, bottom declining)	

Note:
Each of these patterns may occur in either the rising or falling position.

Diagonals

An additional classification of triangles, the diagonals, may also appear in the charts during an impulsive move. The diagonal triangle appears in one of two positions: ascending or descending.

Diagonal triangles most frequently occur in the wave 4 position of either a five-wave impulsive move, or in the wave 4 position of wave C in an A-B-C correction. They are less frequent in the wave 4 position of wave A of an A-B-C correction.[4]

When diagonal triangles, also known as "wedges," occur in the ascending, or rising, form they frequently presage a retracement to approximately the base of the wedge after breaking out from the "apex," or tip, of the wedge. In the descending, or falling, form wedges also normally point to a retracement of the entire wedge before prices continue on in their prevailing direction.

Diagonals

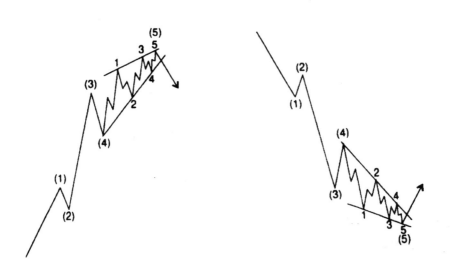

Extensions

Occasionally, what Elliott called an "extension" may develop within a wave progression. Extensions-which are always composed of five waves-may develop in either a 1st wave, a 3rd wave, or a 5th wave of an advancing or declining sequence. Note the examples below:

Extension

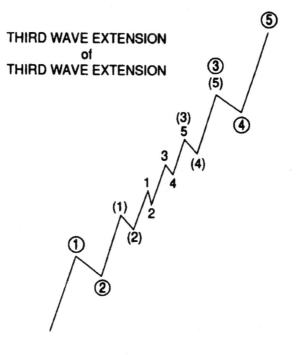

THIRD WAVE EXTENSION
of
THIRD WAVE EXTENSION

Truncations

A truncated, or abbreviated, wave progression occurs when wave 5 in either an ascending or descending price sequence is cut short and fails to progress above the preceding wave 4. Such instances are rare, but when they do occur it signals that either a market has prematurely lost strength and momentum (as in the case of a rising market that has developed a truncated wave 5) or that a market that was previously weak has suddenly gained buying interest (as in a falling market that has developed a truncated fifth wave).

Truncations

Bull Market Failure

Bear Market Failure

Notes:

[1] Prechter, Robert, *The Basics of the Elliott Wave Principle*, New Classics Library, Gainesville, Ga., 1995, pg. 25
[2] Ibid, pg. 25
[3] Ibid, pg. 27
[4] Beckman, Robert, *Elliott Wave Explained: A Real-World Guide to Predicting & Profiting from Market Turns*, Probus Publishing, London, 1995, pg. 163

Chapter 4

Pitfalls of the Elliott Wave Theory

Before we proceed further in our understanding of Elliott Wave Theory we think it only fair and necessary to point out certain pitfalls and failures in the theory. Our encomium of Elliott must be tempered with criticism, and this will provide the basis for this chapter.

The first objection normally voiced against the reliability of the Wave Theory is that it is mechanistic—that is, it attempts to analyze and forecast crowd behavior (through the medium of the stock market) while treating the psyche of the investing public that it attempts to analyze as a machine or robot. Richard D. Wyckoff, writing under the nom de plume of Rollo Tape in his 1910 classic, *Studies in Tape Reading*, summarized the market best when he observed: "The market is made by the minds of many men. The state of these minds is reflected in the prices of securities in which their owners operate.[1]

It has long been a criticism that Elliott Wave Theory treats the market, and by extension the millions of operators who compose it, as a gigantic machine. Furthermore, it is charged by Elliott's critics that besides being mechanistic, the theory is deterministic in that it designs to offer an explanation for the overall movements of the market before they even occur. As we shall see, this charge is not entirely without merit.

One of the most forthright charges against the theory by Elliott's critics is that the entire five-wave impulsive structure of market swings is non-existent. "The problem with this general market concept is that, most of the time, there are no regular 5-wave swings," writes Robert Fischer in his book, *Fibonacci Applications and Strategies for Traders.* "More often, the 5-wave swing is the exception."

Continues Fischer:

The Elliott Wave principles are brilliantly conceived. They work perfectly in "regular" markets and give stunning results when looking back at the charts. The most significant problem is that market swings are irregular. This makes it difficult to give definitive answers to questions such as:

• Are we in an impulsive wave or corrective wave?
• Will there be a fifth wave?
• Is the correction flat or zigzag?
• Will there be an extension in wave 1,3, or 5?

Elliott said, "The Principle has been carefully tested and used successfully by subscribers in forecasting market movements."[2] In another place he mentioned, "hereafter letters will be issued on completion of a wave and not await the entire cycle. In this matter, students may learn how to do their own forecasting and at no expense. The phenomenon and its practical application become increasingly interesting because the market continually unfolds new examples to which may be applied unchanging rules."[3]

As Fischer points out, the Wave Principle does have its shortcomings, particularly in the area of wave counting. It cannot be denied that wave counts are often confusing and do not always develop along the 5-3-5 pattern outlined by Elliott. Fischer proposes to solve this problem by heavy reliance on Fibonacci ratios, an adjunct to the Wave Theory that we will not address here due to its complex nature. Our experience shows that neither a strict interpretation of the Wave Principle's basic rules nor a reliance on Fibonacci ratios is necessary for profitably exploiting the Elliott Wave Theory. Our simplified version of the Wave Principle is the subject of this book, and we will uncover the details of it in the pages that follow.

Probably the greatest pitfall of the Wave Principle is one that is built in. Since EWT by its very nature tends to focus the analysts' attention on the individual fluctuations of a price movement, regardless of how small, it becomes very easy to "get lost" in the wave count while simultaneously missing the bigger picture. For this reason we recommend disregarding the smaller fluctuations altogether, as we will explain later.

The Elliott Wave Theory is a marvelous tool for forecasting price movements in various markets. However, its drawbacks lie in its inherently rigid wave-counting structure and, when followed mechanically, it tends to produce frustration on the part of the analyst. With the right adjustments, however, these pitfalls can be avoided. Our goal in writing this book is to show you how this may be accomplished.

Notes:

[1] Tape, Rollo, *Studies in Tape Reading*, Publishing Concepts, 1910, reprinted in 1999, 816 Easely St., #411, Silver Spring, MD 20910, pg. 38

[2] Hill, J.R., *The Complete Writings of R.N. Elliott with Practical Applications from J.R. Hill*, Commodities Research Institute, 1979, pg. 107

[3] Fischer, Robert, *Fibonacci Applications and Strategies for Traders, Wiley,* 1993, pgs. 21-22

Chapter 5

Elliott Wave
and Technical Analysis

A full comprehension of the Elliott Wave Theory is impossible without a grounding in the basics of classical technical analysis. In its most basic form, technical analysis is nothing more than the forecasting of price trends based on chart pattern recognition. Since Elliott Wave Theory is also based on pattern recognition, basic technical analysis serves as an excellent complement.

Chart patterns form the backbone of technical analysis because they succinctly let the analyst know what is happening in the market at any given time. Technical analyst Ralph Bloch sums it up nicely: "[Chart patterns] are either accumulation patterns, continuation patterns, or distribution patterns."[1]

One of the most fascinating aspects of the Wave Theory is that it records-with pictorial simplicity-the collective emotional impulses of the masses of investors. The very designation "wave theory" draws a parallel between the rhythmic movements of the vast ocean and the rhythmic, wave-like mass emotions of the crowd as they register in the ripples and thrusts of the stock chart.

It has long been observed that the ocean waves that hit the beach have a triple rhythm.[2] The great ocean waves, it is claimed, reach the coast in threes: "Three great waves, then an indeterminate run of lesser rhythms, then three great waves again."[3] The implication, therefore, is that the Elliott Wave Theory is based upon a principle found in nature consisting of alternating rhythms or currents that occur with predictable regularity. We will have more to say of this "rule of alternation" in a later chapter.

The point we are trying to make is that the Wave Principle, like nature itself, is simplicity personified. Any attempt that is made to truly understand the Wave Principle can only be done within the context of this simplicity. We will begin our simplified approach with a number of basic chart techniques.

Trendlines

The first of these techniques involves the use of the most basic and simple of all technical tools—the trendline. One of the tenets basic to technical analysis is that prices move in trends, and that these trends tend to continue until acted upon by strong, opposite forces. Understanding this basic principle alone will give the technical analyst a major advantage over anyone using fundamental analysis.

There are only three types of trends a market may take: up, down, or sideways (horizontal). It remains up to the analyst to determine which of these three trends is in place at any given time. Admittedly, this is sometimes a difficult task since the primary, or major, trend may be up while prices may take a temporary downward path only to resume the previous uptrend once the "correction" is over. A major goal, then, of technical analysis (and Elliott Wave analysis) is to determine price trends and identify turning points in the market.

How, then, are we to approach this task? The most simple and effective way is through the use of trendlines, that is, a perfectly straight line drawn on the chart connecting either the bottoms (troughs) of prices (in order to determine an uptrend) or the tops (peaks) of prices (in order to determine a downtrend). As Edwards & Magee put it:

If we actually apply a ruler to a number of charted price trends, we quickly discover that the line which most often is really straight in an uptrend is a line connecting the lower extremes of the minor recessions within those trends. On a descending price trend, the line most likely to be straight is the one that connects the tops of the minor rallies within it, while the minor bottoms may or may not fall along a straight edge.[4]

Trendlines

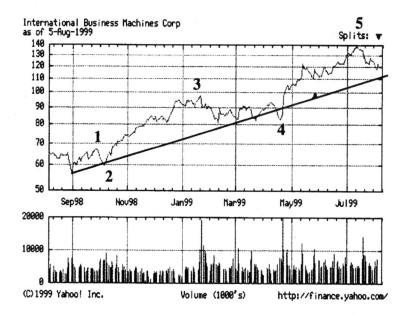

Trendlines

Phlx Gold & Silver Index
as of 6-Aug-1999

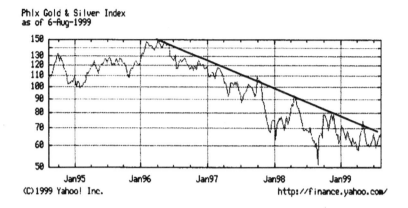

Trendlines whether in the upward or downward-slanting position, cannot be drawn arbitrarily but must correspond to a basic set of rules. One of these rules—given by Edwards & Magee—is that a straight line is mathematically determined by any two points along it. "In order to draw a trendline, therefore, we require two determining points-two established top reversal points to fix a down trendline and two established bottom reversal points to fix an up trendline."[5]

One of the most useful purposes of a trendline is in establishing reversals or turning points in the trend. Reversals are indicated by a break below (or above, as the case may be) the trendline by at least 3 percent (the "three percent rule"). [As an aside, it may be worth noting that legendary trader Jesse Livermore, in his book, *How to Trade in Stocks* (Traders Press, 1993), affixed an almost mystical value upon the number three in his market analysis. Instead of using a filter of 3 percent as Edwards & Magee advocate, he urged the use of a 3 point filter, regardless of what price the security in question is trading at. In today's marketplace that rule may or may not be valid, but at least one leading technical analyst, Kenneth Shaleen, author of *Volume and Open Interest* (Irwin, 1996) asserted that this rule may still be used in future markets analysis].

The three percent rule must be strictly adhered to, for sometimes prices do break above or below a trendline only to recover and continue along the previously established trendline. A break of 3 percent or more, however, is very likely to represent a true turnaround of the trend.

Edwards & Magee give us two more useful rules for identifying turning points when using trendlines:

When the trendline is broken (i.e., when prices drop down through it in decisive fashion), it signals that the advance has run out. It calls time for the intermediate-term trader to sell out that issue, and look for reinvestment opportunities elsewhere.

When a small top reversal pattern [such as a head and shoulders, for instance] forms on the chart of an issue well up and away from that issue's intermediate up trendline, so that there apparently is room for the downside implications of the reversal formations to be carried out before the trendline is violated, then the intermediate-trend trader may well decide to ignore the small reversal pattern. He can hold on so long as the trendline holds.[6]

Of course, volume of trading activity (as with any technical measure or chart pattern) can and should be used to confirm the validity of a trendline breakthrough. As always, a noticeable increase in volume adds more weight to the legitimacy of any such trendline penetration. A trendline penetration occurring on conspicuously high volume, even when the 3 percent rule has not been satisfied, is often enough to qualify as a change of trend, and the trader should respond accordingly.[7]

Edwards & Magee provide further tests which may be applied to judge the technical validity, or authority, of an uptrendline:

1. The greater the number of bottoms that have developed at (or even near) a trendline in the course of a series of minor up waves, the greater the importance of that line in the technical sense. With each successive "test," the significance of the line is increased.

2. The length of the line, i.e., the longer it has held without being penetrated by prices, the greater its technical significance. If your trendline is drawn from two original bottoms which are very close together in time—say, less than a week apart—it is subject to error; it may be too steep or (more often) too flat. If the latter, prices may move away from it and stay high above it for a long time; they may then turn down and have declined well along in an intermediate correction before the trendline thus drawn is reached. But if the trendline has been drawn from bottoms which are far enough apart to have developed as independent wave components of the trend you are trying to define, with a good rally and "open water" between them, then it is more apt to be the true trendline. Greater weight should be given to the number of bottoms that have formed on a trendline (Test A) than to its length alone (Test B).

3. The angle of the trendline (to the horizontal) is also, to some degree, a criterion of its validity as a true delimiter of intermediate trend...Steep lines are of little forecasting value to the technician. The flatter, more nearly horizontal the trendline, the more important it is technically and, in consequence, the greater the significance of any downside break through it.[8]

Further expounding on the principle of the angle of the trendline, Edwards & Magee point out that intermediate uptrends on the daily charts, "in the great majority of issues selling in the 10 to 50 range, rise at an angle of approximately 30 degrees to the horizontal. Some will be a trifle flatter, some a trifle steeper, but it is surprising to see how often the trendline falls very close to the 30-degree slope in stocks of average volatility and activity[9] As a corollary to this, it must be point-

ed out that this applies only to charts made on semi-logarith-
mic scale.

From an Elliott Wave perspective, the trendline can be an
important tool for determining at what juncture the current
cycle is in. As long as a definite trendline can be drawn on a
chart, it provides a strong indication that a five-wave impulsive
move is underway. As long as the trendline remains unviolated
(meaning that no penetration has occurred) an analyst can
assume the current impulsive wave series is still in force and
will continue in the direction of the trendline (whether up or
down) until a violation occurs. The exception to this rule is
when a fourth wave (regardless of degree) partially violates a
trendline only to return back above it. This is actually a common
occurrence with fourth waves and should not be interpreted as
the beginning of a correction (and hence a new trend).

Elliott Wave Pattern Along Trendline

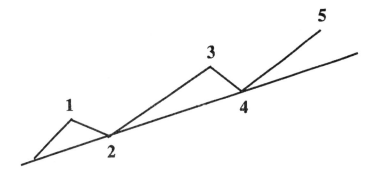

This raises the question, "How does one tell whether a trend-line penetration is merely a fourth wave or the start of a new one?" This can best be answered by the use of "filters." A filter in technical analysis is a rule used to filter out insignificant (and misleading) fluctuations, thereby making price analysis easier. A good rule of thumb for using trendline filters is the venerable "three percent rule" mentioned previously in this chapter. As long as the price does not penetrate three percent or more below the trendline, the trendline should be considered to be intact. Of course, some markets are more volatile than others and the analyst is urged to use discretion according to the character of the market he is dealing with. In some securities, for instance, where trading tends to be extraordinarily volatile, it may be appropriate to use a filter of 10 percent or even higher. A working knowledge of a given security's history is obviously useful in deciding what kind of filter to use.

A further advantage of the trendline to the Elliott Wave analyst is that it tends to simplify wave counting. Under most circumstances each wave trough (in an uptrend) or wave crest (in a downtrend) should touch the trendline before bouncing higher or lower (as the case may be).

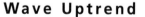 **Wave Uptrend**   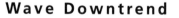 **Wave Downtrend**

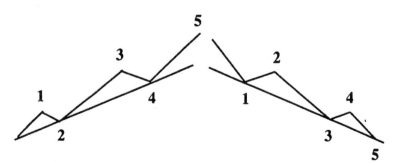

In this chapter, we have addressed the use of the trendline with an eye toward analyzing short and intermediate-term trends. The trendline concept works equally well for analyzing trendlines of larger degrees. In the grand scheme of a given market's progress, there will likely be many trendlines identifiable at various levels within the larger trend. Some will be of minor significance while others will be of greater importance in the longer term. With practice, an analyst will learn how much weight to assign to each trendline and which ones to attach significance to. Ultimately, it remains up to the analyst to decide since much depends on his investment time frame, whether short, intermediate or long-term.

Notes:

[1] Wilkinson, Chris, *Technically Speaking*, Traders Press, Greenville, S.C., 1997, pg. 62
[2] Murphy, John, *Technical Analysis of the Futures Markets*, New York Institute of Finance, 1986, pg. 377
[3] Ibid, pg. 377
[4] Edwards & Magee, *Technical Analysis of Stock Trends*, Amacom, New York, 1996, pg. 283-4
[5] Ibid, pgs. 284-5
[6] Ibid, pg. 289
[7] Ibid, pg. 296
[8] Ibid, pgs. 291-92
[9] Ibid, pg. 293

Chapter 6

The Fan Principle

In the previous chapter we examined the use of the basic trendline in technical analysis and its Elliott Wave applications. The subject of our present chapter is closely related to the trendline, and many analysts treat it as a subset of trendline analysis. For our purposes, however, we will treat it as a separate and distinct classification and will affix to it its own chapter heading. The Fan Principle, the subject of this chapter, is of such great importance that we consider it to be one of the most significant principles in technical analysis. If you learn nothing else from this book, learn the Fan Principle—it will take you far as a trader or investor.

The Fan Principle is used primarily as an identifier and indicator of corrections and trend reversals. Proper implementation of this rule will allow the analyst to catch most trend reversals of minor, intermediate, and primary significance.

In its simplest form the Fan Principle, also known as "fan lines," is a measure of percentage retracement. Specifically, fan lines measure the percentage retracement of the first, second, and third reactions in a correction within a trending market. In its more complex form, fan lines are drawn in strict accordance with the Fibonacci "Golden Ratio" principle, which states that a correction should approximately retrace 0.38 percent (one-third) and 0.618 percent (two-thirds) in its secondary and tertiary retracements. See the chart on the following page for an example of the fan line principle.

Fan Lines

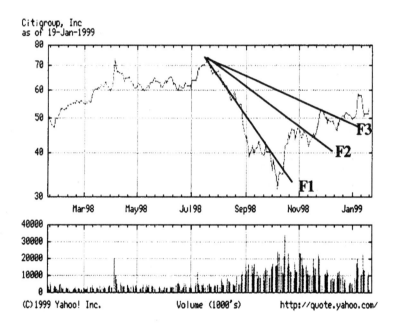

Most Elliott Wave analysts insist on drawing fan lines only when a precise one-third:two-thirds relationship can be seen in price reactions on the chart. We postulate, however, that a strict adherence to Fibonacci ratios is not necessary in fan line construction since markets generally retrace according to these ratios, anyway, and can be seen on the charts in the form of support and resistance levels without having to construct theoretical Fibonacci lines. Furthermore, it must be remembered that market retracements are not always precise that cannot be expected to always conform to Fibonacci measurements. Fortunately, it is not necessary to understand Fibonacci ratios when performing market analysis, (although some Elliott analysts would argue otherwise). The charts almost always make it easy on the analyst when it comes to fan line construction.

Edwards & Magee had this to say about the Fan Principle:

In a bull market, it starts with a sharp reaction which proceeds for several days—perhaps for as much as two weeks—producing a steep minor trendline. This line is broken upside by a quick minor rally, after which prices slide off again in a duller and less precipitate trend. A second minor trendline may now be drawn from the original high point across the top of the upthrust that broke the first rend. This second trendline is broken by another partial recovery thrust, and a third and still duller and flatter sell-off ensues. A third trendline can now be drawn from the original high across the top of the second upthrust. The whole move, by this time, has taken roughly and irregularly a "saucering-out" form. The three trend lines drawn from the original reversal point from which the corrective decline started, each at a flatter angle than its predecessor, are known as fan lines. And the rule is that when the third fan line is broken upside, the low of the intermediate correction has been seen.[1]

According to Edwards & Magee, the purpose of the fan principle is to determine the end of intermediate reactions in a bull market and of intermediate recoveries in a bear market.[2]

However, the Fan Principle can be used as a tool for determining changes in the trend at minor and major points, as well.

Fan lines are most helpful to the Elliott Wave analyst when used to determine if a new impulsive trend has started, or if the correction of the existing trend is only temporary. The basic rule to remember is that a mere correction will stop short of breaking below (or above, depending on the direction of the trend) the trendline, but an actual change in trend will break above (or below) it.

Trend Change Under Fan Principle

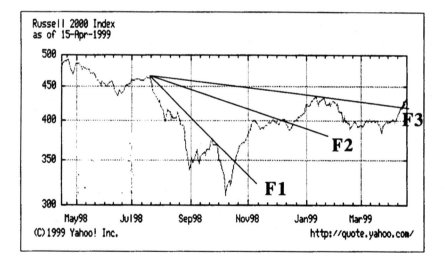

Following are several examples of the Fan Principle in action taken from real-time charts.

Fan Principle in Real-Time

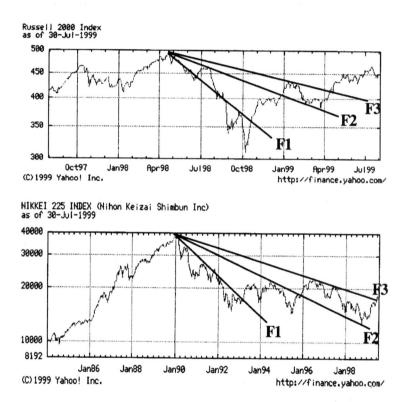

Notes:

[1] Edwards & Magee, *Technical Analysis of Stock Trends*, Amacom, New York, 1996, pg. 313
[2] Ibid, pg. 314

Chapter 7

Elliott Wave
and Channel Analysis

In this chapter we will discuss a technical formation known as a channel, which is most commonly seen in actively traded securities of with a large number of outstanding shares (and least often in the less popular, thinly-traded equities which receive only sporadic attention from traders). The channel plays an important role in both classical technical analysis and Elliott Wave Theory.

Edwards & Magee define a channel for us in the following terms:

In a fair share of normal trends...the minor waves are sufficiently regular to be defined at their extremes by another line. That is, the tops of the rallies composing an intermediate advance sometimes develop along a line which is approximately parallel to the basic trendline projected along their bottoms. This parallel might be called the return line, since it marks the zone where reactions (return moves against the primary trend) originate. The area between basic trendline and return line is the trend channel.[1]

Prices bound by trend channels follow the Rule of Alternation in which a move that meets with the top of the channel line elicits a bounce to the bottom line and vice-versa in a repeating pattern (we will have more to say about the Rule of Alternation in the next chapter).

Channel

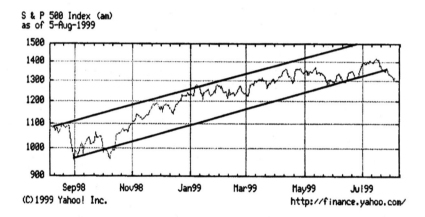

The trend channel played an important role in the original development of the Elliott Wave Theory. In *The Wave Principle*, the first of R.N. Elliott's works, published in 1938, Elliott states, "To properly observe a market's movements, and hence to segregate the individual waves of such a movement, it is necessary that the movement, as it progresses, be channeled between parallel lines."[2]

As a general rule, one should always wait for the completion of the first two waves in a beginning impulsive move before drawing a trend channel. A trend channel cannot be formed until the first two waves of a cycle are complete.[3]

Robert Beckman, author of *Elliott Wave Explained*, describes the construction of the Elliott Wave trend channel in the following terms:

When preparing the channel, a tangent, which will be referred to as a base line, should be drawn using the contact points of 0 and 2. Once this base line has been drawn, a line parallel to it should be drawn, using 1 as the contact point, and extended some distance to the right (as shown in the example on the following page). This line will establish the upper limits of the trend channel.

It will also be found useful to draw a trend line tangential with the bottoms of the entire first-wave movement, subsequently using contact 2 as a point from which to draw a further line parallel to the trend line, between 0 and 1. The upper trend-channel line will help establish probable targets relative to the size of the succeeding waves; the channels within the channel will help establish time-frame references. These channels have been labeled A and B.

A further line has been drawn between contact points 1 and 2. This line has been established by using the peaks of the downtrend between 1 and 2, whereas the trend line between contact points 0 and 1 has been formed by drawing a line tangential to the bottoms of the uptrend. Generally, when drawing trend lines we use the troughs as tangent points in an uptrend, and the peaks as tangent points in a downtrend.

Elliott Wave Channel Construction

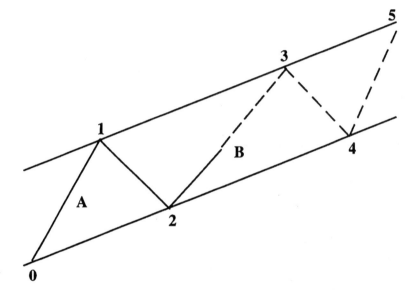

We can now establish a probable target for the end of the third wave in price and time, based on normal, market-behavior patterns.

Assuming that normal, market behavior continues and the third wave terminates at the top of the trend channel, at the price and time coordinate established, one can then use the channel for plotting the possible termination in price and time for the fourth and fifth waves. Using the end of the third wave as contact point 3, one draws a line parallel to that drawn between contact points 1 and 2. The point at which this line contacts the bottom of the trend channel will establish a probable price target and date of termination for the fourth wave.

In the same manner, once the fourth wave has been completed, and a contact point formed, a line is drawn parallel to the first and third waves. The point at which this line touches the top of the trend channel will provide the target for the fifth wave in both price and time.[4]

Beckman notes that in employing the channeling technique, normal behavior indicates that wave 3 of a movement should terminate in the vicinity of the upper trend channel line that was drawn upon completion of the first two waves of the movement. "Should wave 3 end above the upper limits of the trend channel, the movement has taken on temporary strength, and therefore modifications to the trend-channel structure should be made. In the event Wave 3 terminates below the upper limits of the trend channel, a failure occurs, and once again adjustments must be made.[5]

Beckman continues:

The question then arises: When drawing a hypothetical Wave V, what references are used?...The answer can be found in the normal characteristics of wave relationships. According to Elliott, the dimensions of Wave V should resemble those of Wave I in both price and time.

Therefore, in constructing our hypothetical Wave V, we connect the top and bottom of the trend channel by drawing a line parallel to Wave I, which gives us the minimum probable extent of Wave V, both on the price coordinate and the time coordinate.

Elliott Wave Channel Construction

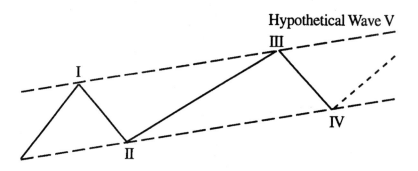

Elliott observed further characteristics of market behavior which extend the concept even further. These characteristics were noted with particular regard to the most important movement of the bull market, the final fifth wave. Normally, the fifth wave will terminate at the top of the trend channel; therefore, establishing targets at that level will, on most occasions, prove helpful.[6]

Notes:

[1] Edwards & Magee, *Technical Analysis of Stock Trends*, Amacom, New York, 1996, pg. 313
[2] Beckman, Robert, *Elliott Wave Explained: A Real-World Guide to Predicting & Profiting from Market Turns*, Probus Publishing, London, 1995, pg. 97
[3] Ibid, pg. 103
[4] Ibid, pgs. 103-4
[5] Ibid, pg. 105
[6] Ibid, pg. 106

Chapter 8

The Rule of Alternation

Elliott Wave Theory is based on the "Rule of Alternation." Simply stated, this means that in financial markets—and in all of the created universe, for that matter—every action has an opposite action, or reaction.

In its application to technical analysis, this rule was probably first observed and applied by George Cole, who wrote a seminal work on technical analysis entitled, *Graphs and Their Application to Speculation.* Although Cole had a different name for it, he gave the following description of it:

According to the Law of Action and Reaction, frequently the market reverses and makes what might be called secondary runs of good proportions, either up or down, in opposition to the primary trend, which ends in a congestion. Then, after working in the level attained within a limited movement up and down for more or less time, it will move out of the congestion in a movement of approximately the same extent, in the same direction against the primary trend, or reverse, going with or against the primary trend for a distance approximately equal to the first "secondary run."

It is obvious that in every second reverse the movement is in the same direction as and comparatively parallel with the original movement. The theory is that the extent of every parallel movement, regardless of the trend of the market, should be equal to the last movement in the same direction. This is according to the Law of Recurrence.[1]

Rule of Alternation in Action

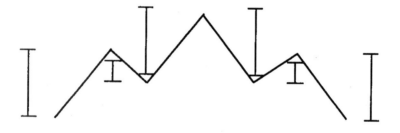

The application of the Rule of Alternation to the Elliott Wave Theory is obvious, for the theory itself is based on this rule. Wave 1 will be followed by wave 2 in the opposite direction, followed by wave 3 in the opposite direction to wave 2, and so on. Further, the individual waves themselves carry minimum measuring implications which can be used to approximate the extent of future waves. For instance, waves 1 and 3 usually approximate in both length and duration, as do waves 2 and 4, regardless of whether the waves are in the impulsive or corrective position. The same normally holds true for all three waves of a typical A-B-C correction. Observes Robert Beckman in *Elliott Wave Explained:*

Elliott's Theory of Alternation has a number of basic applications, the most obvious being the manner in which first wave formations alternate with three-wave formations when a bear market follows a bull market and corrective action follows impulsive wave action. According to R.N. Elliott, form, balance, symmetry, and alternation are a "law of nature" and are inviolate. Leaves on the branches of trees appear first on one side of the main stem and then on the opposite side, alternating their position. Alternation occurs in galaxies, flowers, sea shells, and bumps in pineapples, and was fundamental to Niels Bohr's discovery of the process of cognition. Alternation, in the geo-political science, was an inherent feature of Oswald Spengler's finding in Decline of the West. Kepler tried to describe the distances between two planets as a system in which bodies are alternately inscribed and circumscribed in spheres. There is an endless list of examples that can be offered by nature and the sciences which support the principle of alternation. But, the object of this exercise is the pattern of alternation as it is reflected in human activity. With human activity, we have continuous alternation with little alteration.

Autumn follows summer, night follows day, famine follows feast, bear markets follow bull markets, and yang follows yin. Bull markets and bear markets alternate. A bull market is composed of five waves and a bear market of three waves. Five and three alternate-this same rule governs all the degrees, from the most minute to the most grandiose over time.

Within the five-wave upward movement, Waves I, III, and V are in an upward direction, and waves II and IV are in a downward direction. Within three waves of a downward movement, the first wave is downward, the second wave is upward, and the third wave is downward. The first wave of a downward movement will have Waves 1, 3, and 5 traveling in a downward direction, while Waves 2 and 4 travel in an upward direction. Up alternates with down. Odd numbers alternate with even numbers.[2]

Notes:

[1] Cole, George, *Graphs and Their Application to Speculation*, Pitman Publishing, London, 1998, originally published in 1936
[2] Beckman, Robert, *Elliott Wave Explained: A Real-World Guide to Predicting & Profiting from Market Turns*, Probus Publishing, London, 1995, pgs. 191-92

Chapter 9

Elliott Wave and Volume Analysis

We come now to one of the most overlooked measures in technical analysis—trading volume. In recent years, market technicians—including Elliott Wave analysts—have largely ignored this crucial market gauge in their examination of the market, instead preferring to focus solely on price. Indeed, even Elliott himself made scant reference to volume in his writings. This is a mistake, and one that has been largely responsible for the perceived "failure" of the Elliott Wave Theory. For without taking into account volume into one's market analysis, the analyst comes away with only half the picture. Volume is to price what gasoline is to a car, and you cannot have one without the other. With a proper understanding of volume, however, the Elliott Wave Theory takes on new life, and one's analysis of the market becomes much more accurate.

What constitutes volume? Quite simply, volume is the total number of contracts (or shares) traded during a single trading session or over a given period of time. As a technical indication, volume provides important clues as to investor sentiment, the level of commitment (or non-commitment) of traders to a given market trend, as well as what is happening within a given chart pattern.

As a rule, volume should expand in the direction of the price trend. If the prevailing trend is up, volume should be heavier on the up days and lighter on the down days. If the trend is down, volume should be heavier on the down days, with lighter volume on the up days. This is because in an uptrend there should be more buyers than sellers, and in a downtrend there should be more sellers than buyers. If volume should start to diminish, it could be a warning that the trend could be losing steam and that a consolidation or perhaps a reversal could be ahead. If the trend was up, and we now see more volume on dips than on rallies, it should be an alert that buying pressure is waning and sellers are becoming more aggressive. The reverse would be true in a downtrend. If volume starts to shrink on the sell-offs and picks up on the rallies, once again, it could be a sign that the trend is in trouble, and buyers are starting to assert themselves. When volume moves in the opposite direction of the price, this is called divergence.

One of the reasons why volume has a tendency to diminish during periods of indecision is for just that reason. During periods of lateral movement on the charts, traders will often avoid the market, preferring to commit their funds only when a clear-cut breakout is seen. However, while it is typical for volume to diminish during such times, volume can give the analyst clues as to possible near-term direction by measuring the level of conviction of the buyers and sellers. Seeing if there is heavier volume on the up days or on the down days, the buyers are probably the more aggressive, and the market should break out to the upside. The reverse being true on the down days, the market should break to the downside.

Addressing the relation of volume to price movements, Robert Rhea, in *The Dow Theory*, wrote:

A market which has been overbought becomes dull on rallies and develops activity on declines; conversely, when a market is oversold, the tendency is to become dull on

*declines and active on rallies. Bull markets terminate in a
period of excessive activity and begin with comparatively
light transactions.*[1]

He states further:

*Examination of the daily movements of the averages and
volume trading over a long period of years demonstrates
that the tendency is for volume to increase whenever new
highs or new lows have been made in primary bull or bear
markets, with such an increase frequently progressing until
something like a climax indicates a temporary reversal of
the movement.*[2]

Rhea concludes:

*In emphasizing the importance of volume, the writer does
not, of course, intend to convey the idea that volume of trading is as important as the movements of the industrial and
transportation averages. The latter are always to be considered as of primary importance. Volume is of secondary significance, but it should never be overlooked when a study is
being made of the price movement.*[3]

Martin Pring, in *Technical Analysis Explained*, expounded
upon the traditional concept of volume as a price trend corrob-
oration by demonstrating it can also serve as a price indicator.
Quoting William Gordon, author of *The Stock Market
Indicators*, he writes:

*In 84 percent of the bull markets the volume high did not
occur at the price peak but some months before.*[4]

Pring notes that volume "has an almost consistent tendency
to peak out ahead of price during both bull and bear phases."[5]
He concludes that volume "gives strong indications of a trend
reversal when it moves in the opposite direction to the prevailing trend."[6]

Addressing the subject of volume from an Elliott Wave point of view, Robert Beckman in *Elliott Wave Explained* writes:

According to Elliott, there is a relatively consistent relationship between the pattern of volume, the characteristics of the impulsive waves, and corrective waves of an uptrend. Any deviation from these characteristics should be regarded with suspicion.

During the course of a major five-wave uptrend, volume will tend to gradually increase during the course of the first wave of the cycle, contract during the second wave of the cycle, expand during the third wave of the cycle, contract again during the fourth wave, and be reaching new cycle highs during the fifth and final wave. Further highs will be recorded if the fifth wave becomes extended.

As the five-wave cycle progresses, the volume during Wave 2 should be far less than that which was seen during Wave 1. The volume levels recorded during Wave 3 should be greater than those of Wave 1. Volume levels during Wave 4 should be less than those recorded during Wave 3, but greater than that of Wave 2. The volume of Wave 5 should be the highest of the cycle, although rare, when the volume during Wave 5 has been greater than Wave 3. (see example below)

The illustration demonstrates the manner in which volume levels should be expected to continue to advance during Waves 1 and 3, but become somewhat labored during the course of Wave 5. Also note that although the level of volume should contract during Wave 4 of the sequence, even at the terminal point of Wave 4, volume is still comparatively high.

Typical Elliott Wave Volume Pattern

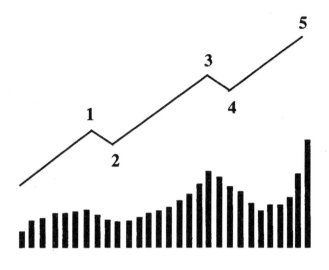

In general, during the course of an ongoing bull market, volume and price should agree in their general direction. When the market rises, the level of volume should also rise. When the market falls, the level of volume should contract. As long as the level of volume continues to expand, and there is no divergence between price and volume, one can assume a further advance in the price action is likely.

When the fifth and final wave is reached, volume divergences will begin to appear. If the level of volume continues to rise while the price action suddenly turns lethargic, you are being warned that an important reversal is in the offing. When the price action starts to advance, but volume does not, the uptrend move is nearing an end.[7]

As an aside, we would note that Elliott adds a note of caution about markets, when the level of volume is extremely low

"...when markets are abnormally 'thin,' the usual volume signals are sometimes deceptive."[8]

Rounding out our study of volume in Elliott Wave patterns we list the following summary of considerations an analyst should be cognizant of when performing volume analysis:

• At any given point in time, markets are either under distribution or accumulation, which involves random trend persistency of a stochastic nature. Shifts in supply or demand characteristics, as expressed by changes in volume trends, can often give warnings of current or approaching trend reversals.[9]

• A rise in volume levels is a normal expectation following a break above the upper parameters of a triangle or a flat; following a period of low activity; when a market breaks above an historic high; or when corrective action has been completed or is drawing toward completion. Heavy volume under any other conditions is likely to indicate a reversal of the prevailing trend.[10]

• When volume expands as the price action declines, this is characteristic of a liquidating market. The downtrend is likely to continue until there is a reversal in the volume relationship. An approaching end to the downtrend is indicated when the level of volume begins to contract as the market falls and expands on rallying action.[11]

• A sharp one-day rally on low volume indicates short covering. The price levels achieved are unlikely to be maintained.[12]

• Following a day when there is exceptionally high volume, be on the alert for the possibility that either a buying climax or a selling climax has occurred. If volume refuses to expand within three days of the suspected climax, the climax will have been confirmed.[13]

• The breaking of the apex of a triangle on heavy volume is significant, indicating the corrective pattern has been completed.

A break of a triangle on low volume is not significant, indicating the pattern is likely to extend.[14]

• The breaking of the resistance level of a flat on high volume is significant. If a break occurs on low volume, it becomes likely that the price action will return to the confines of the flat.[15]

• During a rising impulsive wave, it is a sign of weakness if volume continues to expand while the price action begins to narrow. Under these circumstances, supply can be seen to be gradually exceeding demand. If the level of volume continues to rise while thrusts become increasingly powerful, this is a sign of strength, since demand under such conditions will be exceeding supply.[16]

• Approaching the end of a corrective phase, it will be a sign of strength when volume begins to increase while the price action narrows. This type of action will often be the precursor to a final low-volume Wave 5 of Wave C before the next upswing.[17]

• Heavy volume is constructive, provided there is a continuation in the trend of the price movement and the price movement does not re-enter a corrective flat or a triangle following a bulge in volume levels. If there is a re-entry into a congestion range following a high-volume upward thrust, this would follow distribution and be a sign of weakness.[18]

Notes:

[1] Rhea, Robert, *The Dow Theory*, Fraser Publishing, Burlington, VT, 1993, pg. 86

[2] Ibid, pg. 89

[3] Ibid, pg. 92

[4] Pring, Martin, *Technical Analysis Explained*, McGraw-Hill, New York, 1993, pg. 273

[5] Ibid, pg. 273

[6] Ibid, pg. 288

[7] Beckman, Robert, *Elliott Wave Explained: A Real-World Guide to Predicting & Profiting from Market Turns*, Probus Publishing, London, 1995, pgs. 201-2

[8] Ibid, pg. 203

[9] Ibid, pg. 204

[10] Ibid, pg. 204

[11] Ibid, pg. 204

[12] Ibid, pg. 204

[13] Ibid, pg. 204

[14] Ibid, pg. 205

[15] Ibid, pg. 205

[16] Ibid, pg. 205

[17] Ibid, pg. 205

[18] Ibid, pg. 205

Chapter 10

Elliott Wave
and Contrary Opinion

One area of market analysis that has come to be relied upon as a useful adjunct to technical analysis is the use of sentiment indicators. In using such indicators the analyst attempts to obtain a grasp of the predominant psychology of the market and use this to formulate a trading approach based on contrary opinion. The premise for this branch of technical analysis (though it is more "psychological" than "technical") is that at any given time the majority of traders and investors are on the wrong side of the market. Indeed, Elliott Wave Theory is itself contrarian in nature.

Another assumption underlying this form of analysis is that spotting divergences of opinion among traders is helpful for gaining an understanding of where the market may be heading. "What is important to understand," wrote Kenneth Shalleen in his book, *Volume and Open Interest*, "is that the difference of opinion [among traders] creates a market that can sustain a significant price move."[1] Without this all-important difference of opinion, or sentiment, trading activity comes to a standstill and it becomes exceedingly difficult to make money. This is why being able to gauge market sentiment is so important.

Martin Pring, in *Technical Analysis Explained*, gives us further insight into this subject:

During primary bull and bear markets the psychology of all investors moves from pessimism and fear to hope, overconfidence, and greed. For the majority the feeling of confidence is built up over a period of rising prices, so that optimism reaches its peak around the same point that the market is also reaching its high. Conversely, the majority is most pessimistic at market bottoms, at precisely the point when it should be buying. These observations are as valid for intermediate-term peaks and troughs as they are for primary ones. The difference is normally of degree. At an intermediate-term low, for example, significant problems are perceived, but at a primary market low, they often seem insurmountable. In some respects the worse the problems, the more significant the bottom.

The better-informed market participants, such as insiders and stock exchange members, tend to act in a manner contrary to that of the majority by selling at market tops and buying at market bottoms. Both groups go through a complete cycle of emotions, but in completely opposite phases. This is not to suggest that members of the public are always wrong at major market turns and that professionals are always correct; rather, the implication is that, in aggregate, the opinions of these groups are usually in direct conflict.[2]

While the measurement and quantification of investor sentiment may seem a dubious prospect, successful attempts have been made and the process of gathering, interpreting, and extrapolating investment trends from such data has become refined in recent years to the point of almost being a science. While many avenues exist for obtaining such data, the source most heavily used by U.S. investors is *The Bullish Consensus*, published by the Market Vane Advisory Service. Each week a poll of market letters is taken to determine the degree of bullishness or bearishness among commodity professionals. The rationale behind this approach is that most traders and investors are influenced to a great extent by market advisory services. By monitoring the views of the professional market letters, therefore, a reasonably accurate gauge of the attitudes of the trading public can be obtained.[3]

The method for interpreting these numbers is fairly simple. If the number of bullish advisors is above 80%, the market is considered to be overbought and implies that a top may be near. A reading below 30% (meaning that only 30% are bullish and 70% are bearish) is interpreted to warn of an oversold condition and the increased likelihood that a market bottom is near.

Commenting on this principle, John Murphy, author of *Technical Analysis of the Futures Markets*, writes:

...if 80% to 90% of market traders are bullish on a market, it is assumed that they have already taken their market positions. Who is left to buy and push the market higher? This then is one of the keys to understanding Contrary Opinion. If the overwhelming sentiment of market traders is on one side of the market, there simply isn't enough buying or selling pressure left to continue the present trend.[4]

Another commonly used sentiment indicator is what is known as the "magazine cover indicator." Used primarily as a turning point indicator, this tool for measuring crowd psychology is helpful for discerning the pulse of the investing public and the likely near-term direction of the market. Martin Pring explains:

The crowd is typically wrong at major market turning points, and the news media normally reflect majority opinion. Therefore, a sentiment indicator based solely on reports, cover stories, network news items, and other public sources would probably be extremely useful. However, a careful study of popular magazine publications (such as Time, Newsweek, U.S. News & World Report, Fortune, and Business Week), the network evening news, financial books on the best seller list, and other such sources can offer a very useful supplement to the indicator approach.

Typically, at the top or bottom of an established move, the story of a market crashing, the gold price soaring, or some other extreme event is in itself newsworthy, and the story will appear as either a prominent article or a cover-story. Unfortunately, by the time the facts have been widely disseminated, they have usually been well discounted by the markets; it is thus much more likely that the media are publicizing the end rather than the beginning of a move.[5]

Pring adds this note of caution, however: "It is very important, therefore, to make sure that such stories are consistent with the other technical indicators."[6]

An option-derived sentiment indicator developed by two leading exponents of the Elliott Wave Theory, Bob Prechter and Dave Allman, compares the open interest on puts and calls on the Standard & Poors (S&P) 100 (OEX). Open interest is the total number of outstanding options at the end of each trading day.

Prechter and Allman use a 10-day moving average of the ratio, which has the advantage of being far less erratic than the actual ratio. However, because the open interest figure is far less erratic than daily volume, there are fewer signals. As a result, the signals are quite useful for identifying intermediate-term as opposed to short-term reversals.[7]

The actual indicator is constructed from a 10-day moving average of daily ratios. A reading of 2.0 in either direction is unusual and typically signals an important turning point in the market. Market bottoms appear to be associated with declines below 0.50.[8] Market peaks, on the other hand, appear to be signaled when the ratio moves above the 1.9 percent level and then falls back below it.

Successful integration of contrary opinion and sentiment indicators can serve as a helpful adjunct to Elliott Wave analysis. Such integration, however, requires the skill that comes with experience. With practice, the Elliott trader should be able to improve the accuracy of his trading by combining Elliott Wave Theory with sentiment indicators.

Notes:

[1] Shalleen, Kenneth, *Volume and Open Interest*, Irwin, New York, 1997, pg. 21
[2] Pring, Martin, *Technical Analysis Explained*, McGraw-Hill, New York, 1993, pg. 353
[3] Murphy, John, *Technical Analysis of the Futures Markets*, New York Institute of Finance, 1986, pg. 316
[4] Ibid, pg. 318
[5] Pring, pgs. 371-73
[6] Ibid, pg. 373
[7] Ibid, pg. 369
[8] Ibid, pg. 370

Chapter 11

Filtered Waves

The Elliott Wave Theory's greatest utility is its uncanny accuracy in highlighting turning points in the market. As a technical tool, Elliott Wave is peerless when it comes to identifying changes in the trend—minor, intermediate, and primary. However, the minor fluctuations and random "noise" generated by the markets sometimes tend to obscure these turning points, making it more difficult for the Elliott analyst to identify these key events. Fortunately, there exists an auxiliary tool to help the analyst filter out the excess noise caused by market volatility— "filtered waves."

The filtered wave concept was developed by Arthur Merril, who outlined this principle in his 1977 book, *Filtered Waves & Basic Theory*. The measuring device described by Merril is an amplitude filter. Waves are measured by the filter required to eliminate them. In simple terms, if an analyst chooses to ignore all swings of less than 6%, he is using a 6% filter.[1]

"The use of a filter permits simplification," says Merril. "Stock market prices move in waves within waves within waves; this can be confusing. If a filter is used, the important swings are clearly evident.[2]

So the first step in constructing a filtered wave chart is to "filter out" all the excess noise and refine the chart until it becomes smoothed out. It is up to the analyst to decide to what degree a chart should be filtered—whether to use a 3%, 5% or 10%—whatever—filter. This decision, however, should not be made arbitrarily but should be based on a variety of important factors, including the time element, the "character" of the stock or commodity being charted, and the degree and magnitude of the trend (whether minor, intermediate, or primary).

Once that has been established the next step in constructing the filtered wave chart can be taken. Merril explains:

The first step is to decide the smallest wave to be charted. This is the filter size. In our studies of the swings of the Dow Jones Industrials...we have used a minimum of 5%.

Suppose, for example, that we use a filter of 5%, and that prices have been rising, and have risen more than 5%. We continue to note new highs made in the swing, and for each new high point achieved, we divide by 105% to get a new reversal signal (RS). Now suppose that prices start to decline. We do nothing until the RS point is reached. When this occurs, we know that we have been in a qualifying decline since the last high point. This establishes the high point as a qualified turning point which can be plotted on a chart.

In graphic form, the situation is this:

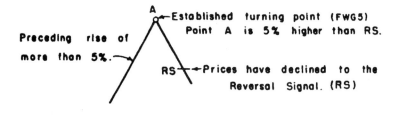

Preceding rise of more than 5%.

A
← Established turning point (FWG5)
Point A is 5% higher than RS.

RS **→ Prices have declined to the Reversal Signal. (RS)**

Merril continues:

Now that prices are declining, new low points are noted. As each new low point is made, it is multiplied by 105%, to get a new reversal signal (RS). If prices turn around and start upward, nothing is done until the RS level is reached. When this occurs, the preceding low point is established as a qualifying turning point, and can be plotted on a chart. The situation is as follows:[3]

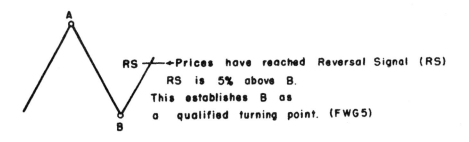

A

RS **→ Prices have reached Reversal Signal (RS)**
RS is 5% above B.
This establishes B as
a qualified turning point. (FWG5)

B

Waves are measured by the vertical distance between turning points, expressed as a percent of the lowest point.[4]

Upswings and downswings should be put on the same basis, always using 100% at the lowest point.[5] Merril puts this in perspective with the following analogy: suppose a worker's salary is cut 10% (of the high point) during a recession. Later, when business improves, his pay is increased by 10%. This does not, however, restore his pay cut, since the increase percentage is now based on the low point. Writes Merril:

Before a filterable wave can be measured, it must be identified. Two adjacent turning points may not be a complete swing; they may be part of a larger swing in the same direction. Note this chart:

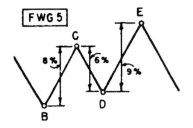 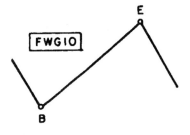

*The left hand chart shows all waves of more than 5%
(FWG5); the right hand chart uses a 10% filter (FWG10).*

*Note that the upswing B-C, although it is only 8%, is not
eliminated by the 10% filter. It is part of the larger upswing B-
E. The same is true of the upswing D-E. The wave C-D, however, completely disappears; it is a filterable wave.*

*The requirements for a complete swing are then evident;
the swing must be smaller than both the previous swing and
the swing which follows.*[6]

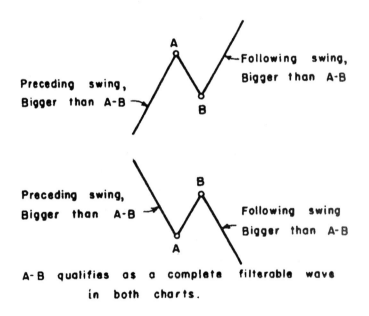

Preceding swing,
Bigger than A-B →

A

Following swing,
Bigger than A-B

B

Preceding swing,
Bigger than A-B →

B

A

Following swing
Bigger than A-B

A-B qualifies as a complete filterable wave
in both charts.

Applying filtered waves to the Elliott Wave Theory can ease the task of wave counting by highlighting turning points, thereby making them easier to identify. Merril explains:

Elliott had some problems in the application of his principle. Many of his turning points were debatable; his wave patterns tend to proliferate into variations.

The selection of turning points is crucial. You can identify almost any pattern if you select the proper turning points. When filtered waves are applied, some of Elliott's turning points appear to be quite light, and he seems to have missed some important turns.[7]

It follows, then, that using filtered waves can greatly aid the analyst in applying the Elliott Wave Theory.

Notes:

[1] Merril, Arthur, *Filtered Waves & Basic Theory*, The Analysis Press, Chappaqua, N.Y., 1977, pg. 1
[2] Ibid, pg. 1
[3] Ibid, pgs. 6-7
[4] Ibid, pg. 8
[5] Ibid, pg. 8
[6] Ibid, pgs. 8-9
[7] Ibid, pg. 170

Chapter 12

Conclusion

There are many applications of the Elliott Wave Theory in the analysis of stocks and commodities. The Elliott Wave Theory is perhaps one of the most important and overlooked techniques in the entire discipline of technical analysis. As it stands in its original form, however, it is in need of refinement and augmentation before it can be practiced with a significant degree of accuracy. Our endeavor in writing this book has been to assist in this refining process, however small our contribution may be. Hopefully, other analysts will follow suit and add their input in reconstructing this most fascinating of technical theories.

In formulating his theory, R.N. Elliott had little to work with in the way of perfecting the guidelines of wave formation in real time. While he was able to backtest his theory to a certain degree, he lived at a time when stock market data was harder to obtain than it is today, and computers were not yet available to assist him in his work. Charts had to be constructed by hand—a tedious task to be sure. This, added to the fact that he was advanced in age and in poor health when he developed his theory, served greatly to hinder the perfectibility of his magnum opus. Had he lived a few more years and had the tools at his disposal that we now take for granted, perhaps Elliott would have worked out the kinks and presented us with a more rounded-out theory. Such, however, was not to be his fate, and while he left us a considerable base on which to build, there is still much to be accomplished in the way of developing the Elliott Wave Theory.

Our primary purpose in writing this book has been to present the rudiments of the Elliott Wave Theory in a manner that can be understood by both layman and professionals alike. We have also endeavored to add a few needed adjustments to the theory. For those who desire a more comprehensive explanation of Elliott Wave we would recommend to you the works of the leading exponents of the theory. Bob Prechter, Glenn Neely, and Bob Beckman are among the most distinguished of these.[1]

In our years of studying the theory and reading the Elliott Wave writings of other analysts we have come to note some conspicuous shortcomings in how most analysts use the theory, and we have addressed some of these problems within this book. Foremost among them is the absence of volume analysis, the failure to integrate basic trendline and chart pattern analysis with Elliott Wave analysis, and the almost obsessional focus on wave counting to the exclusion of the overall position of the market, which is always of paramount importance and is of more value than the individual fluctuations. Though much work remains before Elliott reaches a degree of perfectibility, we believe the information contained in this book will facilitate a greater understanding and skill in the use of this highly known but widely abused technical tool.

If you, the reader, come away from reading this book with nothing else, remember this: the most important thing in the analysis of securities is to concentrate on the overall trend. When consolidations or drawn-out lateral patterns develop within a given market, do not worry about losing count of the waves; instead, focus on the underlying trend as well as any classic chart patterns that may be identifiable. While wave counting is important, it isn't as important as the trend itself, for while prices *generally* adhere to the guidelines of Elliott Wave formation it is doubtful that they always *specifically* adhere to them. Being armed with this bit of information alone will take you far in your study of the markets and will greatly increase the value of your portfolio.

Thank you for buying this book, and we wish you every success in your journey through the marketplace.

Note:

[1] Bob Prechter, president of Elliott Wave International, can be reached at P.O. Box 1618, Gainesville, GA 30503. Glenn Neely, president of The Elliott Wave Institute, can be reached at 1278 Glenneyre St., Laguna Beach, CA 92561. Robert Beckman can be reached through Irwin Professional Publishing, 1333 Burr Ridge Pkwy., Burr Ridge, IL 60521.

Appendix 1

Elliott Wave
and Chart Pattern Analysis

Stock market chart patterns take one of three basic forms: accumulation patterns, distribution patterns, or continuation (a.k.a., consolidation) patterns. Each of these is reflected in the charts as geometric shapes. This is where basic chart pattern analysis derives its fuel. When one learns to recognize these basic patterns, of which there are only three basic categories of patterns, he is well on his way to excelling at technical analysis and at making substantial profits in the stock market.

One major problem that we have encountered through the years of studying Elliott Wave is the prominent disposition among Elliott analysts of giving priority to a particular wave count when it conflicts with a clear-cut chart pattern. For instance, an analyst may label the waves of a downward impulsive trend in a given stock or commodity, say silver for instance, as a five-wave decline with an intermittent A-B-C rally, and then proceed with the expectation that the decline will continue. However, all along a clear "head and shoulders" bottom (otherwise known as a "rounding bottom"), a pattern which projects a bullish trend reversal is forming. Instead of taking this into account when attempting to label the waves, our analyst persists with his bearish count and ignores the bullish implications of the developing head and shoulders bottom, a move he later comes to regret.

This incident actually happened, as one prominent analyst insisted that silver was in the midst of a bearish declining pattern when the evidence actually indicated quite the opposite. See the silver chart on the following page, extracted from the July 1999 *Elliott Wave Financial Forecast*[1] (a highly recommended publication for students desirous of learning the nuances of Elliott Wave in real-time market analysis).

Incorrect Labeling of Silver Chart

As you can see, this analyst chose to label silver's chart as an A-B-C correction, implying wave C would carry prices well below $4.50/oz. Quite clearly, however, a rounding bottom/head and shoulders pattern had developed (one could also see a "diamond" reversal pattern—a variation of the head and shoulders) projecting prices to a minimum target of $6.50/oz., if not higher, based on the measuring implications of that pattern. Obviously, such an implication would entail a revision of one's wave count (and to his credit, this analyst did later revise his wave count to reflect this).

In writing this our intent is not to berate the skill of this particular analyst, for he is a fine analyst who normally is quite accurate in his market judgment. Even the best "Elliotticians" make mistakes. The point we are trying to make is that one should never allow himself to be "wedded" to a particular wave count when the overriding implication of a given chart pattern contradicts that wave count. In other words, chart patterns should *always* take precedence over wave counts whenever the two conflict. If Elliott Wave practitioners would begin to embrace this rule it would transform Elliott Wave analysis and bring it one step closer to perfection.

This chapter is not meant to provide an overview of basic chart pattern analysis-that would be beyond the scope of our present work. For that, we would point interested readers to our earlier work on the subject, *Technical Analysis Simplified.*[2]

Anyone who is not familiar with basic chart pattern construction should definitely take time to learn it before proceeding further in his study of Elliott Wave Theory.

Notes:

[1] *The Elliott Wave Financial Forecast*, P.O. Box 1618, Gainesville, GA 30503, $233/12 issues

[2] Droke, Clif, *Technical Analysis Simplified,* Publishing Concepts, 816 Easely St., #411, Silver Spring, MD 20910, $16

Appendix 2

Wave Charting

While the charting applications of the Elliott Wave Theory are many and varied, there exists certain obstacles to performing an accurate Elliott analysis in the charts of certain stocks and commodities, particularly, when those securities are illiquid (i.e., not widely held or actively traded). A safe rule of thumb for discerning which securities can be analyzed with Elliott Wave is to deal only in those issues with at least 100,000 shares outstanding and preferably a million shares or more outstanding.

An even better way to exact a thorough wave analysis is to measure the waves on a stock or commodity sector, rather than on individual issues. Since any given sector contains a number of issues, identifiable waves will almost certainly register on the charts of the various sector indexes. One way of obtaining these results is through a practice known as "wave charting."

This groundbreaking technique was invented by a pioneer of technical analysis, Richard W. Wyckoff. The technique involves the averaging of the leading stocks in a given sector. Jack Hutson, in *Charting the Stock Market: The Wyckoff Method*, explains:

A wave chart shows the psychological moment to buy or sell. It is the pulse of the market, a condensed picture of every vital development in every stock market session and an invaluable aid in determining the turning points of minor and intermediate swings-frequently days before the popular averages give an indication.

Wave charts are graphs of the aggregate price of the five leading stocks of an industry group over the past several months. This group of five is adjusted from time to time, so the wave chart shows the progress of stocks with continuous and real leadership. Every change in the aggregate price throughout the trading day is plotted, and a complete wave chart also shows volume and an index of activity, or intensity, of trading.[1]

As an example, a wave chart of the Internet sector could theoretically be constructed by averaging the daily (or hourly) prices of the five most actively traded Internet stocks. Accumulative daily volume for these five stocks would be averaged as well. This provides a unique and highly reliable medium for spotting Elliott Wave trends in a given sector since they are more likely to be spotted in an aggregate stock chart and are less likely to be influenced by volatility and other ephemeral factors that may produce misleading signals in the chart of an individual stock. As Hutston observed:

Just keep in mind that when you're charting, you're dealing with waves. Every swing in the market, no matter how many points it is, consists of numerous buying and selling waves. The waves last just so long as they can attract a following and when that following is exhausted, the wave ends and a contrary wave sets in. It's much like the tide moving to a higher or lower level through a series of surges.[2]

So, too, is the nature of the Elliott Wave Theory.

Notes:

[1] Hutson, Jack, *Charting the Stock Market: The Wyckoff Method*
Technical Analysis of Stocks & Commodities, 1998, pgs. 22-23
[2] Ibid, pg. 23

Chapter 13

Dictionary of Technical Terms

Accumulation

The first phase of a bull market. The period in which far-sighted investors begin to buy shares from discouraged or distressed sellers. Financial reports are usually at their worst and the public is completely disgusted with the stock market. Volume is only moderate but beginning to increase on the rallies.

Accumulation/Distribution

Momentum indicator that associates changes in price and volume. The indicator is based on the premise that the higher the volume that accompanies a price move, the more significant the price move.

Advance/Decline line

The advance/decline line is undoubtedly the most widely-used measurement of market breadth. It is a cumulative total of the advancing/declining issues. When compared to the movement of the market index, the A/D line has proven to be an effective gauge of the stock market's strength. The A/D line has to confirm the market movements.

The A/D line is calculated by subtracting the number of stocks which declined in price for the day from the number of stocks which advanced, and then adding this value to a cumulative total.

Advisory services

Privately circulated publications which comment upon the future course of financial markets and for which a subscription is usually required.

Evidence suggests that the advisory services in aggregate act in a manner completely opposite to that of the majority and therefore represent a indicator of a contrary opinion. Advisory Sentiment Index = percentage of bullish market newsletter writers in relation to the total of all those expressing an opinion.

Amplitude of cycle

Normally the amplitude of a cycle is a function of its duration; i.e. the longer the cycle the bigger the swing.

Arithmetic scale

All units of measure on an arithmetic scale are plotted using the same vertical distance so that the difference in space between 2 and 4 is the same as that between 20 and 22. This scale is not particularly satisfactory for long-term price movements, since a rise from 2 to 4 represents a doubling of the price whereas a rise from 20 to 22 represents only a 10% increase.

Bear market

Period in which there is essentially a long decline in prices interrupted by important rallies, usually for a long time. Bear markets generally consist of three phases. The first phase is distribution, the second is panic and the third is akin to a washout. Those investors who have held on through the first two phases finally give up during the third phase and liquidate.

Bear spreading

The short sale of a future or option of a nearby month and the purchase of a distant contract. (One notable exception to this principle in the traditional commodity markets is the precious metals group. Bull and bear markets in gold, silver and platinum are led by the distant months.)

Bear trap

Corrections in a bear market which can easily be confused with a reversal or a new bull market. If you are not careful, you can be washed out by a bear trap.

A signal which suggests that the rising trend of an index or stock has reversed, but which proves to be false.

Bull market

A period in which prices are primarily rising, normally for an extended period. Usually, but not always, divisible into three phases. The first phase is accumulation. The second phase is one of a fairly steady advance with increasing volume. The third phase is marked by considerable activity as the public begins to recognize and attempt to profit from the rising market.

Bull trap

A signal which suggests that the declining trend of an index or stock has reversed, but which proves to be false.

Bull spreading

The purchase of a nearby futures/options contract and a short sale of a distant contract. In certain types of bull markets which are caused by a tightness in the supply/demand situation, the nearby contract months usually rise faster than the distant ones.

Beta

Measurement of sensitivity to market movements.

The trading cycle (four weeks) breaks down in two shorter alpha and beta cycles, with an average of two weeks each (Walt Bressert).

Blow-offs

(Climatic top) A sharp advance accompanied by extraordinary volume; i.e. a much larger volume than the normal increase which signals the final "blow-off" of the trend. This is followed either by a reversal (or at least a period of stagnation, formation or consolidation) or by a correction.

Bond market sector

The bond market (i.e. the long end) has three main sectors, which are classified according to issuer.

- US government
- Tax-exempt issuers (i.e. state and local governments)
- Corporate issuers

Breadth (Market)

Breadth relates to the number of issues participating in a move. A rally is considered suspect if the number of advancing issues diminishes as the rally develops. Conversely, if a decline is associated with increasingly fewer falling stocks, it is considered to be a bullish sign.

Breakaway gap

The hole or gap in the chart which is created when a stock or commodity breaks out of an area pattern (areas on the bar chart where no trading has taken place). This gap usually occurs at the completion of an important price pattern and usually signals the beginning of a significant market move.

Breakaway gaps usually occur on heavy volume. More often than not, breakaway gaps are not filled.

Breakout

When a stock or commodity exits an area pattern.

Buying pressure

Buying or selling pressure is measured by volume indicators. It measures the strength of the buying or selling.

Call options

Options which give the buyer the right to buy the underlying contract or stock at a specific price within a certain period and which oblige the seller to sell the contract or stock for the premium received before the expiration of the designated time period.

Cash index

Index expressed in money. This is in contrast to futures prices.

Channel lines

The channel line, or the return line as it is sometimes called, is a line parallel to the basic trend line. It is the line in a bull market which is drawn parallel to the basic uptrend line which connects the lows.

Coils

Another word for a symmetrical triangle. A symmetrical triangle is composed of a series of two or more rallies and reactions in which each succeeding peak is lower than its predecessor, and the bottom of each succeeding reaction is higher than its predecessor.

Commodity options

A commodity gives the holder the right, but not the obligation, to purchase (a call) or sell (a put) on an underlying futures contract at a specific price within a specific period of time.

Composite market index

Composite average - A stock average comprised of the stocks which make up the Dow Jones Industrial Average (DJIA) and the Dow Jones Utility Average.

Basically a market index composed of a selection of specific stocks.

Confirmation

In a pattern the confirmation is the point at which a stock or commodity exits an area pattern in the expected direction by an amount of price and volume sufficient to meet minimum pattern requirements for a bona fide breakout. This is also true for oscillators. To confirm a new high or a new low in a stock or commodity, an oscillator needs to reach a new high or low as well. Failure of the oscillator to confirm a new high or a new low is called divergence and would be considered an early indication of a potential reversal in direction.

Congestion area

The sideways trading area from which area patterns evolve. Not all congestion periods produce a recognizable pattern however.

Consolidation

Also called a continuation pattern, it is an area pattern that breaks out in the direction of the previous trend.

Contrary opinion

A measure of sentiment is useful in assessing the majority view, from which a contrary opinion can be derived.

Cycles

The prices of many commodities reflect seasonal cycles. Due to the agricultural nature of most commodities, these cycles are easily explained and understood. However, for securities the cyclical nature is more difficult to explain. Human nature is probably responsible.

Decennial pattern

A pattern first cited by Edgar Lawrence Smith. It is a ten-year pattern, or cycle of stock price movements, which has essentially repeated itself over a 58-year period.

The decennial pattern can be of greater value if it is used to identify where the strong and weak points usually occur and then to check whether other technical phenomena are consistent.

Diffusion index

A diffusion index shows the percentage of indicators which are above their corresponding levels in a previous period (in this case six months earlier). The indicators are the coincident economic indicators that tend to rise and fall coincidentally with the overall economy. These indicators thus provide a good approximation of the economy. For example: industrial production, consumer installment debt, the federal budget deficit and inflation.

Discount rate

The discount rate is the rate at which banks can borrow directly from the Fed. The Fed can reduce bank reserves by raising the discount rate and expand reserves by lowering the discount rate. In practice the discount rate has little actual influence on interest rates.

Distribution

The first phase of a bear market. During this first phase farsighted investors sense the fact that business earnings have reached an abnormal height and unload their holdings at an increasing pace (accumulation).

Divergence

Divergence refers to a situation in which different delivery months, related markets or technical indicators fail to confirm one another. Divergence is a valuable concept in market analysis and one of the best early warning signals for impending trend reversals.

Diversification

Limiting risk exposure by spreading the investments over different markets or instruments. The more negative the correlation between the markets, the more diversified the risk.

Dominant cycle

Dominant cycles continuously affect futures prices and can be clearly identified. These cycles are the only ones of real value for forecasting purposes. Most futures markets have at least five dominant cycles.

Long-term cycle -----> two or more years in length

Seasonal cycle -----> one year

Primary or intermediate cycle-----> 9 to 26 weeks

Trading cycle-----> four weeks

Short-term cycle-----> several hours to several days

Dow theory

In 1897 Charles Dow developed two broad market averages. The industrial average included 12 blue-chip stocks and the rail average was comprised of 20 railroad enterprises. The Dow theory resulted from a series of articles published by Charles Dow in the *Wall Street Journal* between 1900 and 1902. The Dow theory is the forerunner to most principles of modern technical analysis.

Basic tenets of the Dow theory:

- the averages discount everything;
- the market has three trends: primary, secondary and minor
- major trends have three phases;
- the averages must confirm each other;
- volume must confirm the trend (volume must expand in the direction of the major trend);
- a trend is assumed to be in effect until it gives definite signals that it has reversed.

Downtrend

The trend is simply the direction of the market. A downtrend is a trend that is marked by descending peaks and troughs; in other words, lower subsequent highs and lower lows. An uptrend would be defined as a series of successively higher peaks and troughs (higher highs and higher lows).

Elliott Wave

Theory of market behavior by R.N. Elliott.

Basic tenets of the Elliott Wave principle:

- pattern, ratio and time in that order of importance;
- pattern refers to the wave patterns or formations that comprise one of the most important elements of the theory;
- ratio analysis is useful for determining retracement points and price objectives by measuring the relationship between the different waves;
- and time is used to confirm wave patterns and ratios.

Basic concepts of the Elliott Wave principle:

- action is followed by reaction;
- there are five waves in the direction of the main trend, followed by three corrective waves;
- a 5-3 move completes a cycle. The 5-3 move then becomes two subdivisions of the next higher 5-3 wave; and
- the underlying 5-3 pattern remains constant although the time span of each may vary.
- objectives by measuring the relationship between the different waves;
- and time is used to confirm wave patterns and ratios.

Envelopes

An envelope is comprised of two moving averages. One moving average is shifted upward and the second moving average is shifted downward. Envelopes define the upper and lower boundaries of a stock's normal trading range.

Exhaustion gap

The gap that appears near the end of a market move. Towards the end of an uptrend, prices leap forward with a final gasp. However, this forward leap quickly loses grounds and prices decrease within a couple of days or a week. When prices close under this last gap, it is usually a clear indication that the exhaustion gap has made its appearance. This is a classic example of when the filling of a gap in an uptrend has very bearish implications.

Exponential smoothing

The exponentially smoothed average assigns a greater weight to the more recent activity. It is therefore a weighted moving average. Mathematically, a single exponential smoothing is calculated as follows:

- $X = (C-Xp)K+Xp$

- X is exponential smoothing for the current period.

- C is closing price for the current period.

- Xp is exponential smoothing for the previous period.

- K is smoothing constant, equal to 2/n + 1 for Compu Trac and 2/n for Back Trac.

- n is total number of periods in a simple moving average, which is roughly approximated by X.

Failures

Normally, a failure is when a completed pattern is not confirmed by the direction of the following move. The failure (in the Elliott Wave) shows a situation in which, in a bull market for example, wave 5 breaks down into the required five waves, but fails to exceed the top of wave 3.

Fan lines

Fan lines are constructed as follows:

Two extreme points are identified on the chart, usually an important top and bottom. A vertical line is then drawn from the second extreme to the beginning of the move. This vertical line is then divided by 38%, 50% and 62%, with lines drawn through each point from the beginning of the trend. These three lines should function as support and resistance points on subsequent reactions by measuring 38%, 50% and 62% Fibonacci retracements.

Fibonacci numbers

A number sequence rediscovered by Fibonacci. In Liber Abaci, the Fibonacci sequence is first presented as a solution to a mathematical problem involving the reproduction rate of rabbits. The number sequence presented is 1, 1, 2, 3, 5, 8, 13, 21, 34, 55, 114 and so on to infinity.

In technical analysis, the Fibonacci numbers are used to predict or measure future moves in stocks or to predict retracement levels.

Filter rules

The rule for confirming a breakthrough or a breakout. An example of a filter rule is the 3% penetration criterion. This price filter is used mainly for breaking off longer-term trend lines, but requires that the trend line be broken on a closing basis by at least 3%. The 3% rule does not apply to some financial futures, such as the interest rate markets.

Another example is a time filter, such as the two-day rule.

Flags (continuation pattern)

A flag looks like a flag on the chart. That is, it looks like a flag if it appears in an uptrend. The picture is naturally upside down in a downtrend. It might be described as a small, compact parallelogram of price fluctuations, or a tilted rectangle which slopes back moderately against the prevailing trend.

Flow of funds

Flow of funds analysis refers to the cash position of the different groups, such as mutual funds or large institutional accounts. The thinking here is that the larger the cash position, the more funds which are available for stock purchases. While these forms of analysis are generally considered to be of secondary importance, it often seems that stock market technicians place more reliance on them than on traditional market analysis.

Gann angles

Gann divided price actions into eighths: 1/8, 2/8, ... 8/8. He also divided price actions into thirds: 1/3 and 2/3:

1/8 = 12.5%
2/8 = 25.0%
1/3 = 33.0%
3/8 = 37.5%
4/8 = 50.0%
5/8 = 62.5%
2/3 = 67.0%
6/8 = 75.0%
7/8 = 87.5%
8/8 = 100.0%

The 50% retracement is the most important to Gann. Gann believed that the other percentages were also present in market action, but with diminishing importance.

Gaps

Gaps are simply areas on the bar chart where no trading has taken place. In an uptrend, for example, prices open above the highest price of the previous day, leaving a gap or open space on a chart which is not filled during the day. In a downtrend, the day's highest price is below the previous day's low.

Upside gaps are signs of market strength, while downside gaps are usually signs of weakness.

Group rotation

The overall market consists of many stock groups which are a reflection of the companies making up the various segments of the economy. The economy, defined by an aggregate measure such as Gross National Product (GNP), is either rising or falling at any given time. However, there are very few periods in which all segments are advancing or declining simultaneously. This is because the economy is not one homogeneous unit. Group rotation is the rotation within the different groups of stocks depending on at which stage the economic cycle is at the moment.

Hedging

To obviate risk and avoid speculation. Futures and options can be used for hedging.

High-low indicator

The new high-low cumulative indicator is a long-term market momentum indicator. It is a cumulative total of the difference between the number of stocks reaching a new 52-week high and the number of stocks reaching a new 52-week low. This indicator provides a confirmation of the current trend. Most of the time the indicator will move in the same direction as the major market indices. However, when the indicator and market move in opposite directions (divergence), the market is likely to reverse.

Insiders

Any person who directly or indirectly owns more than 10% of any class of stock listed on a national exchange, or who is an officer or director of the company in question.

Intermediate trend

An intermediate, or secondary, trend is the direction of the trend in a period from three weeks to as many months.

Intra-day

A record of price data during the day, such as 15-minute bar charts. These intra-day charts are extremely important for the timing aspects of trading.

Key reversal day

The term "key reversal day" is widely misunderstood. All one-day reversals are potential key reversal days, but only a few actually become key reversal days. Many of the one-day reversals represent nothing more than temporary pauses in the existing trend after which the trend resumes its course. The true key reversal day marks an important turning point, but it cannot be correctly identified as such until well after the fact; that is, not until after prices have moved significantly in the opposite direction from the prior trend.

Kondratieff cycle

The Kondratieff wave, a 54-year cycle, is named after a Russian economist. This is a long-term cycle identified in prices and economic activity. Since the cycle is extremely long term, it has repeated itself only three times in the stock market.

The up-wave is characterized by rising prices, a growing economy and mildly bullish stock markets. The plateau is characterized by stable prices, peak economic capacity and strong bullish stock markets. The down-wave is characterized by falling prices, severe bear markets and often a major war.

Limit move

A move limited by the uptick or downtick rule in commodity trading.

Log scale

Prices plotted on ratio or log scales show equal distances for similar percentage moves. For example, a move from 10 to 20 (a 100% increase) would be the same distance on a log chart as a move from 20 to 40 or 40 to 80.

Long-term cycle

A long-term cycle is basically two or more years in length.

Major market trend

The major market trend is the primary direction of the market. The Dow theory classifies the major trend as being in effect for longer than a year. Futures traders would be inclined to shorten the major trend to anything longer than six months.

Margin

This occurs when an investor pays part of the purchase price for a security and borrows the balance, usually from a broker; the margin is the difference between the market value of the stock and the loan which is made against it.

Margin: commodities versus stocks

The most important difference between stocks and commodity futures is the lower margin requirements on stock futures. All futures are traded at a margin, which is usually less than 10% of the value of the contract. The result of these low margin requirements is tremendous leverage. Relatively small price moves in either direction tend to be magnified according to their impact on overall trading results.

Margin debt

Debt caused by margin requirements

Market averages

In stock market analysis, the starting point of all market analysis is always the broad market averages, such as the Dow Jones Average or the Standard & Poor's 500 Index. A market average is usually an index of the most important stocks in the market or a broad market index that covers 98-99% of the market as a whole.

Member short sale ratio

The member short ratio (MSR) is a market sentiment indicator which measures the short selling activity of the members of the New York Stock Exchange. "Members" trade on the floor of the exchange, either on their own behalf or for their clients. Knowing what the "smart money" is doing is often a good indication of the near-term market direction.

The MSR is the inverse of the Public Short Sale Ratio.

Minor market trend

The minor, or near-term, trend usually lasts less than three weeks and represents shorter-term fluctuations in the intermediate trend.

Momentum indicator

The momentum indicator measures the amount a security's price has changed over a given time span. It displays the rate of change as a ratio.

Most active stocks

The most active stocks are stocks that are traded the most over a certain period. Statistics on the most active stocks are published in the general press on both a daily and weekly basis. Usually the 20 most active stocks are recorded.

Moving average

A moving average is the average of the closing prices of x periods added up and divided by x. The term "moving" is used because the calculation moves forward in time. Moving averages are used to help identify the different kinds of trends (short-term, intermediate medium, etc.).

A smoothing device with a time lag.

The moving average is one of the most versatile and widely used of all technical indicators. Because of the way it is constructed and the fact that it can be so easily quantified and tested, it is the basis for most mechanical trend-following systems in use today.

Moving average crossovers

One method used by technicians in terms of moving averages. A buy signal is produced when the shorter average crosses above the longer-term moving average. Two popular combinations are the 5 and 20-day averages and the 10 and 40-day averages.

Neckline

Support or resistance level in a Head & Shoulders pattern. The neckline connects the lows or highs of the "shoulders" depending on the situation (H & S bottom or top formation).

Nominality

The principle of nominality is based on the premise that, despite the differences which exist in the various markets and allowing for some variation in implementing cyclical principles, there seems to be a set of harmonically related cycles that affect all markets. A nominal model of cycle lengths can be used as a starting point for any market.

Odd-lot ratios

There are a few odd-lot ratios:

- Odd-lot balance index (OLBI)
- Odd-lot short ratio
- Odd-lot purchases/sales

The OLBI is a market sentiment indicator that shows the ratio of odd-lot sales to purchases (an "odd-lot" is a stock transaction of less than 100 shares). The assumption is that "odd-lotters," the market's smallest traders, do not know what they are doing.

When the odd-lot balance index is high, odd-lotters are selling more than they are buying and are therefore bearish on the market. To trade contrarily to the odd-lotters, you should buy when they are selling.

On-balance volume

On-balance volume (OBV) is a momentum indicator that relates volume to price. The OBV is a running total of volume. It shows whether volume is flowing into or out of a security. When the security closes higher than the previous close, all of the day's volume is considered up-volume. When the security closes lower than the previous close, all of the day's volume is considered down-volume.

The basic assumption in OBV analysis is that OBV changes precede price changes. The theory is that smart money can be seen as flowing into a security by a rising OBV. When the public then moves into a security, both the security and the OBV will surge ahead.

Open interest

Open interest is the number of open contracts of a given futures or options contract. An open contract can be a long or short open contract which has not been exercised, or has been closed out or allowed to expire. Open interest is really more a data field than an indicator.

Oscillators

Method of creating an indicator. The oscillator is extremely useful in non-trending markets where prices fluctuate in a horizontal price band, or trading range, creating a market situation in which most trend-following systems simply do not work that well.

The three most important uses for the oscillator:

- The oscillator is most useful when its value reaches an extreme reading near the upper or lower end of its bound aries. The market is said to be overbought when it is near the upper extreme and oversold when it is near the lower extreme. This warns that the price trend is overextended and vulnerable;
- A divergence between the oscillator and the price action, when the oscillator is in an extreme position, is usually an important warning signal; and
- Crossing the zero line can give important trading signals in the direction of the price trend.

Overbought level

An opinion on the price level. It may refer to a specific indicator or to the market as a whole after a period of vigorous buying, after which it may be argued that prices are overextended for the time being and are in need of a period of downward or horizontal adjustment.

Oversold level

An opinion on the price level. A price move that has overextended itself on the downside.

Overowned stocks

A stock is overowned when fashion-conscious investors are all interested in buying a certain stock.

Point & Figure

Method of charting prices. A new plot on a P&F chart is made only when the price changes by a given amount. P&F charts are only concerned with measuring price.

P&F charts are constructed using combinations of X's and O's known as "boxes." The X shows that prices are moving up, the O that they are moving down. The size of the box and the amount of the reversal are important.

Primary trend

This is the most important long-term trend. A primary trend usually consists of five intermediate trends. Three of the trends form part of the prevailing trend while the remaining two run counter to that trend.

Public/specialist short sale ratio

It measures the round-lot short selling by the public against the New York Stock Exchange specialists on the floor of the exchange. It pits the smart money against one of the least informed categories of market participants.

Rally

A brisk rise following a decline or consolidation of the general price level of the market.

Reaction

A temporary price weakness following an upswing.

Relative strength (RS)

An RS line or index is calculated by dividing one price by another. Usually the divisor is a measure of "the market," such as the DJIA or the Commodity Research Bureau (CRB) Index. A rising line indicates that the index or stock is performing better than "the market" and vice versa. Trends in the RS can be monitored by moving average crossovers, trend line breaks, etc. in the same way as any other indicator.

Resistance

Resistance is the opposite of support and represents a price level or area over the market where selling pressure overcomes buying pressure and a price advance is turned back. A resistance level is usually identified by a previous peak.

Retracement

Retracements are basically countertrend moves. After a particular market move, prices retrace a portion of the previous trend before resuming the move in the original direction. These countertrend moves tend to fall into certain predictable percentage parameters. The best known application of this phenomenon is the 50% retracement. For example: a market is trending higher and travels from the 100 level to the 200 level. The subsequent reaction very often retraces about half of the prior move.

Seasonal cycle

Seasonal cycles are cycles caused by the seasonal changes in the supply-demand relationship (caused by factors that occur at about the same time every year).

Secondary trend

Secondary trends are corrections in the primary trend and usually consist of shorter waves that would be identified as near-term dips and rallies.

Sentiment indicator

Indicators that measure the market sentiment, such as:

- Specialist Public Ratio
- Short Interest Ratio
- Insider Trading
- Advisory Services

Short interest

The short interest is a figure published around the end of the month citing the number of shares that have been sold short on the NYSE.

Speed resistance lines

Technique that combines the trend line with percentage retracements. The speed resistance lines measure the rate of a trend's ascent or descent (in other words, its speed).

Stock index futures

Futures contract on indices.

Support area

Support is a level or area on the chart under the market where buying interest is sufficiently strong to overcome selling pressure. As a result, a decline is halted and prices turn back up again. A support level is usually identified beforehand by a previous reaction low.

Trend line

A trend line is a straight line drawn up to the right that connects important points in a chart. An up trend line is a line that connects the successive reaction lows, and a down trend line connects the successive rally peaks.

Upside/Downside volume

Measurements of upside/downside volume try to separate the volume into advancing and declining stocks. By using this technique, it can be subtly determined whether accumulation or distribution is taking place.

Volume

Volume represents the total amount of trading activity in that market or stock over a given period.

Whipsaws

Misleading moves or breakouts.

About the Author

Clif Droke is the editor of the weekly newsletters *Leading Indicators* and *Internet Stock Outlook*; and the bi-weekly *Gold Strategies Review*. And he is the author of *Technical Analysis Simplified*. The author also forecast the stock market crashes of 1997 and 1998 using many of the techniques outlined in this book and the newsletters listed above.

Technical Analysis
Resource Guide

SUGGESTED READING LIST

Elliott Wave Principle: *Key to Market Behavior*
by Frost & Prechter

The "Bible" of Elliott Wave from the pioneer in wave analysis. Covers basic principles, details the theory and application of the concepts including: Fibonacci numbers, ratio analysis, time sequence, cyclic analysis, & Kondratieff Wave.
$35.00 Item #T140X-2475

Mastering Elliott Wave
by Glenn Neely

"Provides the most complete explanation of Elliott Wave Theory available..." Originally titled Elliott Waves in Motion, unlocks all the keys to accurate and objective usage of Elliott Wave Theory. Concepts are presented in a step-by-step approach that removes guesswork from wave counting. "A masterpiece."
$95.00 Item #T140X-2490

R.N. Elliott's Masterworks: *The Definitive Collection*
Edited by Robert Prechter

Dive deep into the mind of the genius that created use of the Elliott Wave Principle. This collection includes: The Wave Principle (1938), The Financial World Articles (1939), Selected Essays and more, all with Prechter's commentary throughout.
$29.95 Item #T140X-2435

The Elliott Wave Writings of A. J. Frost & Richard Russell
by Frost & Russell

Read all the Elliott Wave work of two masters in one book!
$89.00 Item #T140X-5711

At the Crest of the Tidal Wave
A Forecast for the Great Bear Market
by Robert Prechter $29.95 Item #T140X-8436

An Introduction to Elliott Wave Principle - Video
by Robert Prechter $195 Item #T140X-3110 120 minutes

Real Time Trading Using Elliott Wave - Video
by Robert Prechter $195 Item #T140X-3124 90 minutes

Technical Analysis From A to Z
by Steven B. Achelis

The creator of the most used Technical Analysis software in the world explains virtually every technical indicator known—over 120—with full descriptions and specific uses of each. On the practical use of technical analysis you won't find a more thorough or affordable work. "An essential addition to any technical library," says John Bollinger, former CNBC host.
$29.95 Item #T140x-2396

Technical Analysis of the Financial Markets
by John Murphy

From how to read charts to understanding indicators and the crucial role of technical analysis in investing, you won't find a more thorough or up-to-date source. Revised and expanded for today's changing financial world, it applies to equities as well as the futures markets.
$70.00 Item #T140x-1023

Technical Analysis & Stock Market Profits
by R. W. Schabacker

Everyone from Edwards & Magee on consider this classic the foundation on which all technical analysis is built. It examines patterns, formations, trends, support and resistance areas, etc— which comprise the basis of modern technical analysis, from the Grandfather of it all, & the former finance editor at Forbes and the New York Times.
$65.00 Item #T140x-8473

Technical Analysis of Stock Trends, 7th edition
by Edwards & Magee

A universally acclaimed classic, updated with the latest data in market performance and trends, on which the foundation of all technical analysis is built. Step-by-step coverage thoroughly explains and applies the current data. Stochastics, trend lines, stops, reversals, support/resistance and tactical usage of each.
$75.00 Item #T140x-2376

Technical Analysis Explained, 3rd edition
by Martin Pring

Covers every aspect of technical analysis. Teaches you to interpret market cycles and select the best performing investments. Pring's classic text covers bar chart basics, moving averages, price patterns, RSI, stochastics and more—to help you build winning portfolios.
$49.95 Item #T140x-2373

Martin Pring's Introduction to Technical Analysis
A CD-rom Seminar and Workbook
by Martin Pring

The foremost expert on technical analysis and forecasting financial markets gives you a one-on-one course in every aspect of technical analysis. This interactive guide explains how to evaluate trends, highs and lows, price/volume relationships, price patterns, moving averages and momentum indicators. The CD-rom includes videos, animated diagrams, audio clips and interactive tests. It's the user-friendly way to master technical analysis from an industry icon.
$49.95 Item #T140x-8521

Using Technical Analysis
by Clifford Pistolese

Technical Analysis for everyone! Easy-to-understand primer explains an array of approaches to analyzing stock market charts: chart patterns, volume analysis, timing tactics, trends and more.
$24.95 Item #T140x-3553

Handbook Of Technical Analysis:
A comprehensive Guide to Analytical Methods, Trailing Systems and Technical Indicators
by Darrell Jobman

An in-depth look at all aspects of technical analysis. The roster of contributors is a "Who's Who" of trading: Wilder on RSI, Schwager on uses and abuses of technical analysis, Pring on momentum, Prechter on Elliott Wave and more. From bar charts to candlesticks, volume to Gann—it's a #1 guide to the profit-grabbing techniques of the masters.
$55.00 Item #T140x-3419

The Arms Index (Trin Index):
An Introduction to Volume Analysis
by Richard Arms, Jr.

Finally, it's updated and back in print! Get an in depth look at how volume not time governs market price changes. Describes the Arms' short term trading index (TRIN), a measure of the relative strength of the volume in relation to advancing stocks against that of declines. Also shows how to use Arms' own system to forecast the price changes of individual issues as well as market indexes. A true trading gem.
$39.95 Item #T140x-3130

Analyzing Bar Charts for Profit
by John Magee

A straightforward guide teaching the timetested approach of using technical analysis to minimize risk and boost profits. From the bar chart "king" you'll learn: Classical chart patterns; How to identify trends and trading ranges; Tops, bottoms and what they mean to your bottom line. Plus, the "Magee Method" of buying/selling. "It's the best explanation of the technical process ever written."
$39.95 Item #T140x-2318

Prechter's Perspective
by Robert Prechter

Robert Prechter on the Elliott Wave Principle, Market Analysis and the Nature of Social Trends. Timeless commentary "reveals the full bounty of the Wave Principle" and shows how it relates to investing and popular culture.
$19.00 Item #T140x-2543

The Visual Investor
by John Murphy

Track the ups and downs of stock prices by visually comparing charts—instead of relying on complex formulas and technical concepts. Introduces readers to Intermarket Analysis—a proven analytical approach based on evaluating the impact different markets have on each other. Includes software demo disks and instructions for using charts and graphs.
$39.95 Item #T140x-2379

New Market Wizards
by Jack Schwager

Meet a new generation of market killers. These hot traders make millions—often in hours—and consistently outperform peers. They use vastly different methods, but share big successes. Now, you can meet them and learn their methods. How do they do it? How can you do it? Learn their winning ways with this bestseller.
$39.95 Item #T140x-2106

The Art of Short Selling
by Kathryn F. Staley

Finally, a book showing how to cash in on this lucrative yet overlooked strategy. Staley explains what it is, how it works, best type of companies to short and never before released methods of the world's top short sellers. There's no better time to position yourself to profit from any stock sell off.
$49.95 Item #T140x-2006

Pattern Price & Time:
Using Gann Theory in Trading Systems
by James Herczyk

Here's the first book to simplify Gann's breakthrough techniques for beating the markets. Also shows how to integrate Gann theory into modem computer charting methods.
$59.95 Item #T140x-8438

Profits in Volume: *Equivolume Charting*
by Richard W. Arms, Jr.

This method places emphasis on trading range and volume considered the two primary factors in technical analysis. They give an accurate appraisal of the supply/demand factors that influence a stock. With this critical factor you can determine if a stock is moving with ease or difficulty and—thereby—make more on-target investing decisions.
$39.95 Item #T140x-6780

Point & Figure Charting
by Thomas J. Dorsey

Here's the first new work on Point & Figure in 30 years. Today's leading expert shows how to use point & figure to chart price movements on stocks, options, futures and mutual funds. Learn to interpret the point and figure charts and recognize patterns that signal outstanding opportunities. Also covers how to combine point and figure with technical analysis for unbeatable success. You can't afford to pass by this valuable trading tool, and Dorsey makes it easier than ever.
$59.95 Item #T140x-2364

Candlestick Charting Explained
by Gregory Morris

Brand new book on this phenomenal indicator takes the guesswork out of candlestick analysis. Go beyond the basic theory to build a thorough system using the latest in computer analysis techniques and to identify trends, patterns, tops, bottoms and more.
$35.00 Item #T140x-2347

The Stock Market Barometer
by William P. Hamilton

Dow Theory Method—often known as the Stock Market Barometer—consistently remains a predictable strategy for forecasting the market. Now, this 1922 classic by the former Wall St. Journal editor, has been reissued with a fascinating new foreword. See how applicable this theory is to predicting—and profiting—from the markets today.
$19.95 Item #T140x-8443

Reminiscences of a Stock Operator
by Edwin Lefevre

Generations of investors have benefited from this 1923 masterpiece. Jack Schwager's new introduction explains why this account of Jesse Livermore, one of the greatest speculators ever—continues to be the most widely read book by the trading community. See why industry insider Martin Zweig says, "I keep a supply for people who come to work for me."
$19.95 Item #T140x-2116

INTERNET SITES

Traders' Library Bookstore
www.traderslibrary.com, The #1 source for trading and investment books, videos and related products.

Clif Droke Web Site
www.tapetellsall.com, This site contains a special section dedicated to forecasting markets using the Elliott Wave Theory. The site also provides market commentary and forecasts based on principles from the author's books including Elliott Wave Simplified and Technical Analysis Simplified. It also provides information about the "lost art" of tape reading, which is simply the interpretation of price-to-volume configurations in stocks and commodities.

Elliott Wave Chart
www.wavechart.com, Examine market analysis based on the predictions of the economist R.N. Elliott. Learn how to use this tool as a guide to trading decisions.

Elliott Wave Charting Association Home Page
www.wavechart.com/HOME.HTM, The Elliott Wave Charting Association provides Elliott Wave charts, Expert System charts with buy/sell signals for the stock market (DJIA), Treasury Bond Market (TYX), and the Gold Market (XAU). Software, investment books, and historical data are also available.

Elliott Wave International
www.elliottwave.com, A premier source of technical analysis information.

Introducing
Clif Droke's ...
LEADING INDICATORS newsletter

Discover **Leading Indicators**—the industry's top technical advisory service. This hard hitting, weekly publication covers the U.S. and global equities and commodities markets from a technical perspective. Each and every week you get thorough—*timely*—coverage of all major stock indices, as well as precious metals markets—using a wide array of technical tools including...

- Basic technical analysis
- Elliott Wave Theory analysis
- Japanese Candlestick analysis
- Dow Theory analysis

Plus, comprehensive analysis and forecasts of the market's near-term and intermediate-term direction—EVERY week, 50 profit-packed issues per year.

Order a no-risk subscription—TODAY!

- -

Cliff Droke's LEADING INDICATORS
Only $144 for 1 year (50 issues)

☐ Yes, enter my subscription for 50 weekly issues of *Leading Indicators* for just $144. I understand that if *Leading Indicators* ever ceases to be profitable reading, I may cancel my subscription and receive a credit or refund on all remaining issues—no questions asked.

☐ Payment enclosed   Send check or money order for $144 U.S.
(Sorry, no credit card orders) to:
Leading Indicators, 816 Easely St., #411
Silver Spring, MD 20910

Name & Title: _____

Company: _____

Address: _____

City: _____ State & Zip:_____

NEWSLETTERS

The Dines Report
Editor, Jim Dines
P.O. Box 22, Belvedere, CA 94920

Dow Theory Letters
Editor, Richard Russell
P.O. Box 1759, LaJolla, CA 92038
$233/36 issues

The Elliott Wave Theorist
Editor, Robert Prechter
P.O. Box 1618, Gainesville, GA 30503
$233/12 issues

INSIIDE Track
Editor, Eric S. Hadik
P.O. Box 2252, Naperville, IL 60567
$179/12 issues

Internet Stock Outlook
Editor, Clif Droke
816 Easely St., #411, Silver Spring, MD 20910
$233/50 issues

InvesTech
Editor, James Stack
2472 Birch Glen, Whitefish, MT 59937

Leading Indicators
Editor, Clif Droke
816 Easely St., #411, Silver Spring, MD 20910
$144/50 issues

The Master Indicator
Editor, John T. Goddess
11371 Torchwood Court, Wellington, FL 33414
$100/24 issues

P.Q. Wall Forecast
Editor, P.Q. Wall
P.O. Box 15558, New Orleans, LA 70175
$198/12 issues

The Reaper
Editor, R.E. McMaster
P.O. Box 84901, Phoenix, AZ 85071
$195/36 issues

Stockmarket Cycles
Editor, Peter Eliades
P.O. Box 6873, Santa Rosa, CA 95406-0873

The Wellington Letter
Editor, Bert Dohmen
1132 Bishop St., Suite 1500, Honolulu, HI 96813
$265/9 months

Free 2 Week Trial Offer for U.S. and Canadian Residents From Investor's Business Daily: